THE GOLDEN AGE

Manuscript Painting at the Time of Jean, Duke of Berry

THE GOLDEN AGE

Manuscript Painting at the Time of Jean, Duke of Berry

MARCEL THOMAS

GEORGE BRAZILLER　　NEW YORK

To the memory of Millard Meiss

Translated from the French by Ursule Molinaro and Bruce Benderson

Published in 1979

For information address the publisher:
George Braziller, Inc., One Park Avenue, New York, New York 10016

Library of Congress Cataloging in Publication Data

Thomas Marcel, 1917—
    The golden age.

    Bibliography
    1. Illumination of books and manuscripts, Gothic.
    2. Berry, Jean de France, duc de, 1340-1416. I. Title.

ND2980.T48   745.6'7'094   79-52172

ISBN 0-8076-0923-4

ISBN 0-8076-0924-2 pbk.

First Printing
Printed by Imprimeries Réunies in Switzerland

DESIGNED BY RANDALL DE LEEUW

CONTENTS

Acknowledgments

The author and publishers would like to express their sincere thanks to the following institutions and individuals who kindly provided materials and granted permission to reproduce them in this volume. The author also wishes to express his special gratitude to Mlle. Marie-Thérèse Gousset and to Mrs. Yolanda Zaluska, for their invaluable assistance in gathering the bibliographical information needed to prepare this volume.

Color Plates

BARCELONA, Archivo Capitular de la S.I. Catedral Basilica de Barcelona, Plate 8 (Photo, Ampliaciones y Reproducciones M A S).

BERLIN, Staatsbibliothek, Preussischer Kulturbesitz, Plate 34.

BRUSSELS, Bibliothèque Royale Albert 1er, Plates 13, 14 (Photos, Bibliothèque Royale Albert 1er).

CAMBRIDGE, The Master and Fellows of Corpus Christi College, Cambridge University, Plate 39.

CAMBRIDGE, The Master and Fellows of Trinity College, Cambridge University, Plate 40.

CHANTILLY, Musée Condé, Plates 26, 27 (Photos, Giraudon, Paris).

CLEVELAND, The Cleveland Museum of Art, Mr. and Mrs. William H. Marlatt Fund, Plate 6.

FLORENCE, Biblioteca Nazionale Centrale di Firenze, Plate 4.

GENEVA, Bibliothèque Publique et Universitaire, Plate 30 (Photo François Martin).

LONDON, Reproduced by Permission of the British Library Board, Plates 23, 38.

LÜNEBURG, (West Germany), Ratsbücherei der Stadt Lüneburg, Plate 35 (Photo, Wilhelm Krensien).

MUNICH, Bayerische Staatsbibliothek, Plate 36.

NEW YORK, The Metropolitan Museum of Art, The Cloisters Collection, Plates 24, 25.

NEW YORK, The Pierpont Morgan Library, Plate 3.

NORWICH, University of East Anglia, Alnwick Castle (Duke of Northumberland Collection) Plate 37 (Photo, A. C. Cooper, Ltd., London).

PARIS, Bibliothèque de l'Arsenal, Plate 19 (Photo, Bibliothèque Nationale, Paris).

PARIS, Bibliothèque Nationale, Plates 1, 2, 5, 7, 12, 15, 16 (a, b, c, d), 17 (a, b), 18, 20, 21, 22, 29, 31, 32, 33. (Photos, Bibliothèque Nationale).

PARIS, Musée Jacquemart-André, Plate 28 (Photo, Musée Jacquemart-André).

VIENNA, Österreichische Nationalbibliothek, Plates 9, 10.

Black-and-White Figures

AIX-EN-PROVENCE, Musée des Beaux-Arts, Figure VI.

BASEL, Kunstmuseum Basel, Kupferstichkabinett, Figure VIII.

CHANTILLY, Musée Condé, Figure VII.

FLORENCE, S. Croce, Figure II.

HELSINKI, National Board of Antiquities, Kansallismuseo, Figure XVII.

LONDON, National Gallery, Figure XVIII.

NEW YORK, The Metropolitan Museum of Art, The Cloisters Collection, Figure XIV.

PARIS, Bibliothèque Nationale, Figures III, IV, X, XII, XV, XVI.

PARIS, Musée du Louvre, Figures I, IX, XI.

RALEIGH, Collection of the North Carolina Museum of Art, Gift of the Samuel H. Kress Foundation, Figure XIX.

SAN GIMIGNANO, Collegiata, Monastero di San Girolamo, Figure V.

WASHINGTON, D.C., National Gallery of Art, Rosenwald Collection, Figure XIII.

INTRODUCTION

Preparing a volume that must find its place within the established framework of a collection places obvious and difficult constraints upon an author. Attempting to evoke in forty images the most prestigious period of illumination—during which dozens, even hundreds, of artists of the first order in every part of Western Europe were creating thousands of small masterpieces, each deserving of its own commentary—might seem an impossible gamble to any expert. Such a limitation will inevitably restrict the selection severely, and thus the final result cannot be other than subjective and arbitrary. Therefore, the reader should expect to find in this volume a symbol rather than a panorama.

With this in mind, we thought it fitting to reserve a substantial place for the production of artists and workshops established at Paris, and among these, for the works executed for Jean de France, Duke of Berry. This concentration may seem excessive to some. If the very title of the present volume deliberately places all the illumination of this period under this prince's aegis, it is, nevertheless, no sign of disregard for those remarkable works which were simultaneously created outside the narrow boundaries of the Kingdom of France, for the benefit of patrons as enlightened as a Giangaleazzo Visconti of Milan, or a Wenceslas of Bohemia. Our apparent injustice is no more than a recognition of the quantitative disproportion between Parisian production and that of the rest of Europe at the beginning of the fifteenth century. It is also an indication of the pre-eminent role played by the Duke of Berry in this blossoming of miniature marvels.

Paris was for some time—and to a greater extent than any other center—a crucible of diverse artistic legacies that formed an alloy which the Germans called the *weicher Stil,* but which we will refer to as the "International Style," a term coined during the last century by Courajod. Our secondary motive for reserving a privileged place for the Parisian manuscripts is that they show how these heterogeneous influences were best harmonized, while still managing to retain many of their distinguishing characteristics. In every case we have tried to underline what the illumination in each country owed to foreign influences and how, because of this, all came to be included in a vast group having, in most instances, no clear territorial confines.

It is obviously impossible to explain the infinitely complex history of European illumination between 1380 and 1420 in a few pages, and a long list of titles and manuscript numbers might quickly become as tedious as it would be needless. That is why we have thought it preferable to include within the forty commentaries accompanying the illuminations — reproduced and grouped according to their regions of origin — certain precise indications concerning their dates and places of origin, as well as the stylistic currents by which they were influenced.

It can be easily understood how such a decision hardly makes it possible to explain in a few lines precisely what produced in Western illumination from the end of the fourteenth century to the beginning of the first half of the fifteenth century, both those elements of homogeneity and of diversity. Nevertheless, we cannot dispense with mentioning the climate within which it was to blossom with a vigor equal only to its splendor.

Princely patronage was undeniably one of the most influential of those diverse socio-economic factors which contributed to the rapid development of the production of luxurious manuscripts. The sudden growth of interest in arts and letters, evinced in some European courts and then, because of their example, among their most prosperous subjects (most particularly in the art of the book, which stood as a connecting link between the two) entailed a considerable demand for a very special product. Such a demand would naturally result before too long in an artistic response as remarkable in quality as it was in quantity.

The major patrons, whose names will be noted here (although there were many more who could be mentioned) were, in general, from the highest rung of the social ladder. These sovereigns, princes of royal blood, important noblemen and high officials, all wielded great power and controlled immense riches. In turn, this made them very confident of themselves and of the values they embodied. More or less consciously they imposed upon their craftsmen a certain tone, a certain courtly elegance, in harmony with their personal tastes and the style of life they all shared. If rivalries, or even conflicts, separated them, they were frequently reconciled by marriages. All of these unions were quite obviously motivated by political considerations in which sentiment played a very minor role. Such arrangements could abruptly open a kingdom or province to exterior influences which are particularly easy to detect in the domain of art.

One such example was the marriage of Jean le Bon to Bonne de Luxembourg that gave the Valois important family ties to the Emperor of Germany, Charles IV, and his son, King Wenceslas of Bohemia. In Milan, Giangaleazzo Visconti wed a sister of Charles V of France, and their daughter, Valentine, married her first cousin, Louis d'Orléans. The union of England's Richard II and Isabelle de France, daughter of King Charles VI and Isabeau de Bavière, marked a brief truce in the Hundred Years' War, and prompted artistic exchanges on both sides of the English Channel. Analogous bonds also existed between the House of France and the Kings of Aragon, and were perpetuated from one end of Europe to the other by a long series of offspring.

Such situations were certainly not new. They had previously furnished the key to many a stylistic evolution which would have otherwise remained inexplicable. But, as we have already noted, art at the beginning of the fifteenth century (and more particularly, the art of the book) happened to be very much in fashion in most European courts. The sumptuously decorated manuscript, eagerly leafed through (sometimes more than it was read) seemed to have become one of the essential attributes of nobility and power. Everywhere, notables were happily seeking in this form of art a reflection of their own personalities—further emphasized through a blatant display of their mottoes, coats-of-arms, crests, and eventually, by inclusion of their own portraits.

Although bibliophilism may not have been an invention of the fifteenth century, it is certainly true that European courts then were more open and responsive than ever before to an art whose delicacy and elegance seemed primarily directed toward a feminine clientele, as was the case in France at the time of Pucelle.[1] It is also interesting to note that at the very moment when it was increasing in number, this new clientele became ever more anxious to intervene in the development of the works it sought. Everywhere active patronage gained momentum, a phenomenon whose importance cannot be stressed enough.

There is, in fact, an essential difference between the true patron, who plays for the artist whom he fosters the role of inspirer as much as that of client, and the simple collector. The latter is, above all, a man who has fallen in love with a certain category of objects—often inherited from the past—which he gathers together for his personal gratification, without taking any part in their creation. Although the basic motivations of the patron may be appreciably the same, they exert in his case a direct influence on the very elaboration of the works of art that he commissions, and which are conceived especially to please him. The more enlightened his taste, the more original will be his aesthetic intuitions and the more profound his imprint upon the art of his time. Consequently, it is not surprising that in the course of a very long life, a patron as lavish, a connoisseur as knowledgeable, as Jean de Berry, should have been able to impart to book illumination (for which he had a veritable predilection) an impulsion and orientation that it would surely never have known otherwise.

It should be noted in this regard that his influence was quite different, and decidedly more profound, than that of his older brother, King Charles V. Although the latter was able to assemble a famous library which was to surpass in both wealth and variety all those known before, he was more concerned with the content of his books than with their decoration. In his cultural policy, (the notion of which he doubtless had, without referring to it as such) art held a relatively minor place. Consequently, his influence upon the evolution of book illumination during this period remained proportionately limited.[2]

For his younger brother, it was a different matter altogether. He was able to discover and draw into his service an entire pleiad of exceptional artists, past masters in every form of expression. Moreover, he managed to influence them with his own conceptions, using his favors as a most powerful goad.

In great measure, Jean de Berry's artistic taste was characterized by his eclecticism. He would encourage and generously subsidize stylistic research as "modern," even as revolutionary, as that of the Limbourgs (Plates 24–27) and, at the same time, would reverently keep in his collections the nearly century-old masterpieces of a Pucelle, whose somewhat "dated" charm was the fruit of a quite different aesthetic attitude. What is more, in his *Grandes Heures*, which he intended as a monument to his own glory (Plate 20), he would go so far as to induce his "workmen" to juxtapose copies of paintings executed some twenty years earlier by the "Master of the *Parement de Narbonne*" (Figure I) and grotesques closely imitating those of Pucelle. And this was to be done in the same volume within which Jacquemart de Hesdin, one of the most original artists of the generation preceding the Limbourgs, was also to execute a whole series of large, full-page compositions!

This exceptional desire for syncretism is an excellent example of a great connoisseur's temperament — one who is able to recognize that all forms of expression can be equally worthy of respect and love, once they have gone beyond the passing fads of snobbism or fashion, and have been put to the service of talent.

Not at all concerned about condensing time in the *Grandes Heures*, Jean de Berry was likewise to abolish considerations of space in *The Très Belles Heures of Notre Dame* (Plates 13 and 14). For its execution, he simultaneously employed the talents of the same Jacquemart, and of an artist whose style betrays an Italian origin.

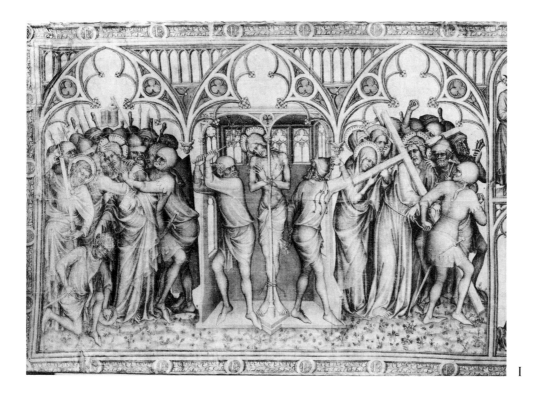

I

His aesthetic curiosity is also revealed in his tendency to have certain of his preferred artists express themselves in unfamiliar media. He would ask a "cutter of images" such as André Beauneveu to paint, in his Psalter, figures of apostles and prophets whose majesty and very coloring startlingly evoke the technique of sculpted statues (Plate 12). In the same spirit, he would make his collection of medallions available to the Limbourgs to allow them to give the Three Wise Men of *The Très Riches Heures* the features and bearing of the Emperors Constantine and Heraclitus, as they appeared on two large medallions that he had acquired several years earlier.[3]

It was to such open-mindedness, and to his ever-alert curiosity, that he owed so much success in his persevering, lifelong search for talent.

However, it should be recognized that, in this respect, the task was a relatively easy one for him. The modest Parisian workshops, struggling at the time to fulfill the demands of an ever-expanding clientele, were staffed with many artists of talent, and even a number of geniuses. Their gifts awaited only the impetus of some lavish commission. Paris was, in fact, the undisputed capital of illumination. But it was a capital which had been open to international influences since the end of the fourteenth century.

This particular phenomenon was of very great importance. Indeed, if the fourteenth century had been marked by the concentration in Paris of il-luminators drawn to the city from the French provinces (as was recently emphasized by François Avril[4]), its final years would see an even greater intensification of the capital's power of attraction — an influence that was to spread throughout Western Europe. The appearance and development of the new style, which was to affect every form of art for the next generation or two, was closely connected to these new conditions.[5]

One of the first and most remarkable manifestations of the new tendencies, imported to Paris by foreign artists, could be noted as early as 1380–1390 in the oldest section of *The Très Belles Heures of Notre Dame*. It is not absolutely certain that this book was commissioned by Jean de Berry, but in any case he was soon to own it, and he ordered its decoration to be continued through several campaigns.[6] The illumination of the volume was originally entrusted both to an unknown master to whom is now generally attributed the famous *Parement de Narbonne* at the Louvre (Figure I), and to an older artist who had previously done much work for Charles V but was then confined to decorating the lower portions of the pages. The style and workmanship of the "Master of the *Parement*" are so strikingly reminiscent of Bohemian painting of the period that it has sometimes been supposed that he was himself of Central European origin, and that the very limited number of his known works could be explained by the brevity of his sojourn in France.

At the time of the death of Charles V, which coincided approximately with the beginning of the execution of *The Très Belles Heures of Notre Dame*, the art of illumination in France was divided between two major trends. One was traditional and continued to follow the path opened at the end of the first quarter of the century by Jean Pucelle, brilliant precursor of Italian painting in France. The other was of Flemish or, if one prefers, Northern, inspiration. It was marked by a vigorous realism which adhered to a representation of every-day life, a painstaking rediscovery of the rules of perspective in order to create the illusion of space, and a substitution of landscapes for conventional backgrounds in exterior scenes.

About ten years later everything was to change. Realism, and all the progress that it implies in the pictorial expression of three-dimensional forms, as well as in the variety and choice of themes, will have overcome the Pucellian mannerisms (whose last rays, however, will brighten certain pages of *The Petites Heures of Jean de Berry* [Plate 15]). But this realism will proceed from a far different and infinitely more eclectic spirit. To Paris then, from Flanders, the Netherlands, Italy, Bohemia, and Germany, will come painters bringing with them memories, processes, techniques, colors — in short, an entire artistic stock-in-trade unknown or disregarded until then. From the confrontation and synthesis of all these legacies, the International Style was to be born and, soon after, re-exported under very diverse and personalized aspects, until it finally imposed itself upon all of Europe.

It is unfortunate that so few precise documents concerning the lives of the illuminators and the organization of their work should have survived. In most instances we are reduced to a study of the work itself when we seek information about those who made it. How we wish we could identify, or even simply enumerate all of these modest artisans! Yet in only a few cases have we been able to lift the veil of their anonymity. From time to time, an account, an inventory, a quotation, or a marginal inscription has been discovered and thus the name of a particular illuminator revealed; seldom, however, can one definite work be attributed to him rather than to another. The abundance of the production permits only the assumption that, at the time, the small "World of the Book" had many citizens (some of whom were women such as that "Anastaise" mentioned by Christine de Pisan). Some artists from Germany or the Netherlands didn't even have to know French to illustrate books written in that language—a few words sketched out by a multi-lingual overseer on the margins of the pages were sufficient to guide their brushes.

If Christine de Pisan is to be believed, the morals and manners of this cosmopolitan milieu were far from exemplary. Carousing and brawls must have been frequent occurrences. We know, for instance, that an unscrupulous plagiarist was quickly repaid with a knife thrust for the theft of a design which had served as a colleague's model.[7] The authorities often had to intervene in the quarter where all the book trades were grouped; and without the opportune intervention of a personage as prominent as the Duke of Berry, one of the Limbourgs would have undoubtedly paid dearly for carrying off a lass of about twelve, despite the fact that he fully intended to make her his legitimate spouse and, in due time, did marry her.

We have very little information about the economic and technical organization of the various professions of bookmaking, especially about the guild of painters and illuminators. The relationship of artist to client, to competitor, associate or subcontractor, and particularly to the "publishers" and copyists who furnished him with work, remains in many respects a mystery. Nevertheless, certain factors can be clearly discerned from a careful study of their work. Notably, we can observe a very pronounced division of work among the various specialists: some were responsible for the margins, others for the backgrounds, some for the rapid placement of the scenes to be represented. Finally, others were charged with a patient execution of the actual paintings. This final phase of the work was often divided among a few collaborators. It will even be possible, in many cases, to distinguish the work of several artists in a single illumination, particularly when it is of large dimensions and especially elaborate.

Such a complex division of tasks obviously implies that there must have been a hierarchy among the executors, and also direction by a responsible overseer, but it would be risky to represent them as always operating under a common "master plan." It is not at all certain that the one habitually referred to as the "head of the workshop" was necessarily the most gifted artist of a team organized like students around a great master. He may often have been only an entrepreneur, who rewarded his salaried collaborators well or poorly, and reserved the right to negotiate their production for his own profit.

One frequently perceives the discreet presence of a more cultured personage in the background, acting as a connecting link among all those whose diverse talents contributed to the execution of a manuscript. An author, publisher, copyist, or combination of all three, he would often take on the responsibility of deciding upon the program of illustration for a new work that did not fit into the relatively unchanging framework of a traditional iconography.[8] We sometimes see that the artist was guided step by step in his work by an unknown hand, of which material traces have been left in the form of brief marginal notes indicating with great precision the details of a scene to be represented or the attitude and costume to be given a particular figure.

Anonymity was the rule in this microcosm, particularly for illuminators employed by commercial workshops. Other than the names of exceptional artists that have been sporadically brought down to us by the accounts of their illustrious clients, and to whom we have painstakingly attributed one volume rather than another, there are many "Masters" whom we have had to invent; and the best of their supposed works will furnish them with only uncertain identities that are constantly being questioned by the specialists.

If we are fortunate enough to possess precise information concerning the lives and careers of the Limbourgs, of André Beauneveu, Jacquemart de Hesdin, Giovannino dei Grassi or Belbello da Pavia, it is due essentially to the fact that at one time or another they entered into the service of a prince who kept an inventory of his collection, or of a religious community with relatively rigorous standards of bookkeeping.

We are, however, completely ignorant of the life, even of the identity, of the "Master of *The Boucicaut Hours*," of the "Master of *The Rohan Hours*," of the "Master of *The Brussels Initials*."

In one manuscript after another, we encounter these enigmatic personalities, sometimes isolated and sometimes associated with one another — most likely because of some intermediary contract. Then suddenly they disappear, without a clue as to whether their careers were interrupted by death or by some other circumstances. How, if not by some unforeseeable accident, could a painter as gifted, talented, and original as the one who began the illustration of *The History of the Jews* (Plate 21) for Jean de Berry have apparently abandoned this project almost immediately? Above all, why should his recorded works, which testify to a mastery impossible to acquire in a short span of time, total no more than the fingers on a single hand?

Perhaps such sudden disappearances could indicate that illumination was only an occasional activity for certain artists. They may have been busy with other "jobs" most of the time, such as the frescoes which then decorated the walls of every princely home but, unfortunately, have not survived. We are certain, at least, that this was true of the Limbourgs and some of Jean de Berry's other "workmen." Neither was such a talent for adaptation among the artists of this period very exceptional. The Limbourgs came to Paris at an early age to serve as apprentices in the workshop of a goldsmith. And, to judge from his very singular technique, the "Master of *The Rohan Hours*" was not only an illuminator, but a fresco painter, and perhaps a designer of tapestries as well. The remarkable facility that fifteenth-century illuminators had for moving at will from one medium to another is one of the principal attractions of their work.

The quality of French artistic production — and more specifically of Parisian illumination — was then an accepted fact among France's neighbors. While a substantial number of foreign painters were bringing new blood to an organism slightly in danger of atrophying, French expatriates were implanting — in countries far from their own homeland — techniques and forms of expression already well established in Paris.

This incessant movement of talent was accompanied, it should be noted, by an even more rapid circulation of themes and motifs. Their exchange and fusion were essential characteristics of the new art as it swept through all of cultivated Europe. The most accomplished of those responsible for its development seem to have had certain qualities in common. In addition to great technical virtuosity, they shared curiosity, a continual availability, and a facility for assimilation that neither personal vanity nor any school of thought or style could curb.

Actually, their versatility was partly (but only partly) imposed upon them by the very nature of the texts they were called upon to illustrate. If religious books, and more specifically, Books of Hours, still constituted a privileged field for the exercise of their talent, they were also asked more and more frequently to apply their gifts to the decoration of secular works. Thus, they were impelled toward new feats of imagination and invention which drew them away from the somewhat too heavily trodden paths of traditional religious iconography.

The need for realism, or verity, that has already been alluded to, urged them to express many aspects of contemporary life for which there were no usable prototypes at that time. Genre scenes full of freshness and animation began to brighten and invigorate works that were often more austere than their illustrations. Around 1405 the works of Boccaccio (only recently translated into French at that time) enjoyed a great vogue. Several skillful artists, guided by an

16

II

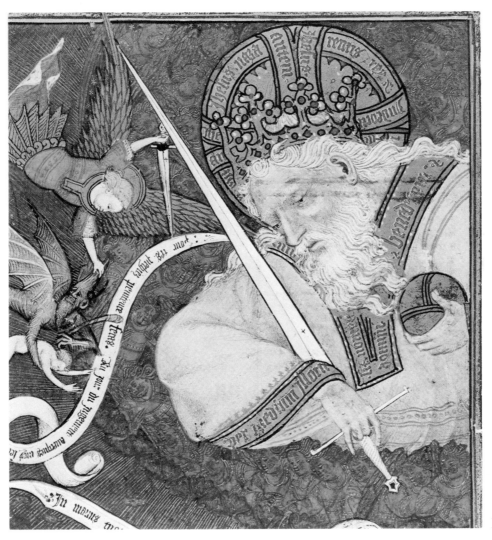

alert overseer, enriched these semi-luxury manuscripts with a long series of enticing little pictures (Plate 16). At the same time, Christine de Pisan directed the illustration of her own works, entrusting them to an artist who, if not Italian, was at least Italianized, and who endeavored to reclothe the mythology of Antiquity in the fashions of the day (Plate 18).

In the dedication copies, portraits that attempted and often attained resemblances, appeared more and more frequently (Plates 13, 15, 20, 23, 30, and 36). This can also be explained by a concern for verity which was evinced by the Limbourg's faithful representations of their master's dwellings in the paintings done for the Calendar of *The Très Riches Heures* (Plate 26). An obvious taste for exoticism was equally expressed in the representation of historical or imagined

V

episodes set in the Orient (Plate 31) or in Antiquity (Plates 19 and 21). Although these representations may seem fanciful to us today because their authors apparently lacked information concerning the times and places they wished to evoke, they were, nevertheless, expressions of a clearly perceived difference between past and present, near and far. Nothing more was needed at the time to elicit a sensation of being removed from familiar surroundings, a sensation of removal as vivid and as enjoyable as that which could be provided by authentic local color.

This penchant for novelty, this desire to depart from the beaten path, expressed itself in the use of models situated so distantly in time and space as to assume, paradoxically, all the value of original creations.

Whether a number of artists born under less clement skies had actually

VI

travelled beyond the Alps, or whether they had studied copies, drawings, or rough drafts, they constantly gave proof of their familiarity with the great Italian painting of the Trecento. In so doing, they were merely following the example of Pucelle and his disciples, who had first introduced indisputably Italian or Italianizing elements into fourteenth-century French illumination.[9] Avignon, where the pontifical court had been established in 1309, served throughout the century as a central launching point for the uninterrupted invasion of France and the Netherlands by the art of Italy. In his works, [10] Millard Meiss brilliantly uncovered an impressive number of tributes by Northern illuminators to their illustrious predecessors. As an example of this, we will mention the relationship he was able to establish between the frescoes of Santa Croce in Florence and the diptych of *The Très Belles Heures of Notre Dame* (Plate 13). The resemblance between the face of the high priest in *The Expulsion of Joachim*, painted by Giovanni da Milano in the Chapel of Rinuccini within this same Florentine Church (Figure II), and that given to God by the "Rohan Master" (Figure III) in his famous *Judgment at Death*[11] must surely have been more than a happy coincidence.

More obvious still is the debt owed to Bartolo di Fredi by the "Master of the *Cité des Dames*" in the latter's *Bible Historiale*. His *Animals Entering the Ark* (Figure IV) was directly derived from a 1367 fresco on the same subject by Bartolo di Fredi in the Collegiate Church of San Gimignano (Figure V). It is not certain, however, whether he actually saw the original with his own eyes, or had recourse to a hastily done rough sketch, which was not exactly identical to

VII

the original, and had been brought back from Italy by a student or admirer of the Sienese master who died in 1410. It is curious, in fact, that the horns of the bovine animal behind the two horses about to enter the ark have the exact sinuosity of the slender necks of two Wading Birds visible in the fresco, but completely absent in the illumination.

This untiring search for famous models sometimes led our innovators in quite unexpected directions. When the opportunity presented itself, they would go very far back to discover sources of inspiration in classical Antiquity that had been forgotten or disregarded for a very long time.[12] One would not wish to go so far as to state that the Limbourgs had before their eyes the Roman statue of a wounded Persian now kept at the Musée d'Aix (Figure VI) when they endowed Adam accepting the forbidden fruit from the hands of Eve in *The Très Riches Heures* (Plate 27 and Figure VII) with the same peculiar pose. Nevertheless, it seems no less certain that this male nude, executed with such exceptional virtuosity, is rooted in the purest tradition of Antiquity. The same could be said about a small number of similar motifs, such as the figures of Gemini in the Calendar of *The Rohan Hours*.[13]

We must point out, however, that this incessant search for themes and motifs was not without its dangers. There was a risk of luring the less inventive illuminators onto the deceptive path of imitation and pastiche, often to the detriment of original creation. The best artists were undoubtedly gifted with temperaments strong enough to bestow upon their works the mark of their own particular genius, even when they borrowed a figure or basic pattern from the work of someone else. This helps us to distinguish them easily from their predecessors and contemporaries. The "*Parement* Master," Jacquemart de Hesdin, the Limbourgs, the "Master of *The Boucicaut Hours*," the "Master of *The Rohan Hours*," Giovannino dei Grassi, and many others, all had personal styles, particular "touches" which could not be confused with any others. Just as Picasso did in his reworking of Velasquez, they knew—even when transposing—how to manifest a very modern taste for what we would today call pictorial "research."

Not all artists had such an elevated conception of their métier, however. The artist of the period was, above all, an artisan—or "workman," as he was then called. As such, he did not necessarily have the special pride in his profession that was to appear later. Art's place in society was still a relatively modest one. None of its practitioners would thus conceive of himself as being invested with any sort of mission. Anxious, above all, to keep his client's favor, the artist strove to furnish that which was expected of him, not to impose any particular aesthetic views—views which, in most cases, he would have had quite some difficulty formulating. To attain his goal—that is to say, quite simply, to make a living—he would accept any opportunity offered him.

VIII

This quite natural desire to satisfy his market with a high output and to thoroughly exploit every profitable vein often caused him to yield to the facility of repetition and re-utilization. (In this respect his technique could be compared to that of today's cartoonist.)

None of those "patterns" traced onto translucent sheets made from a base of glue and gum, which we know illuminators readily used, are still in existence. Various collections of sketches have, however, reached us; some are in the form of albums,[14] others have survived only as separate pages. A series of figures of Madonnas attributed to Jean de Beaumetz and kept today in the Museum of Basel (Figure VIII) allows us to reconstruct in a very precise fashion how these repertoires of forms could have been created and transmitted from one workshop to another, or from master to student; they would always have been available for an artist to use, thus relieving the pressure upon his reserves of imagination.

Self-copying or self-imitation is a largely sterilizing temptation. Artists of every period have occasionally succumbed to it, but in the days of illumination it was a practice which seemed entirely natural. We thus have the advantage today of being relatively confident as to the grouping of particular artists or the attribution of certain works to them. For example, the presence in *The Très Belles Heures of Notre Dame* of a certain group or a figure encountered in the *Parement de Narbonne,* but reduced in the former to the scale of a manuscript page, permits the attributing to a single artist of both a series of illuminations and a vast *grisaille* on canvas destined to decorate an altar. Occasionally, in the two works, it is possible to find identical faces, situated rather surprisingly on different

IX   X

bodies. The gloved soldier who brutally lays hold of Christ in the *Kiss of Judas* in
the *Parement* (Figure IX) reappears in *The Très Belles Heures of Notre Dame* (Figure
X). In both cases the same rictus pulls down the corners of his thin lips.
Likewise, one of the tormentors in the *Flagellation* of the *Parement* (Figure XI)
continues to perform his cruel function in the manuscript (Figure XII). In *The
Très Belles Heures of Notre Dame* he has kept his smock, which draws unchanged
folds against his hips, while the pivot of his torso follows a rigorously identical
angle. Yet, this time, the artist must have wished to profit from the supplemen-
tary expressive facilities color offers, for he gave the figure a black African face,
traditionally intended to inspire terror in subjects of this kind. There is a third
tormentor in the illumination, whereas in the *Parement* there are only two; the
artist borrowed his flat-nosed, brutal face from the figure who offers the sponge
soaked in vinegar to Christ on the Cross in the Crucifixion of the *Parement*.

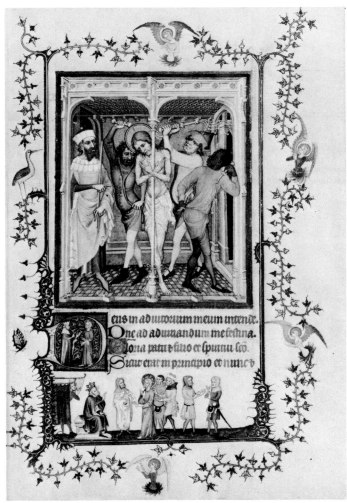

XI

XII

As we have already pointed out, these artists-artisans were not encumbered with our modern scruples in matters of artistic propriety. Without hesitation they resorted to transpositions, as well as to adaptations of their competitors' or masters' discoveries. Possibly this was considered an homage to talent, rather than an act of piracy. The "Master of *The Rohan Hours*" lacked neither individuality nor imagination, yet his borrowings from other illuminators, and notably from the Limbourgs, were extremely frequent. His debt to *The Belles Heures* and *The Très Belles Heures of Notre Dame* is so obvious (among other things, he borrowed the figures of horsemen in pursuit of the Holy Family [Figure XVI], a model created by the Limbourgs for *The Meeting of the Three Wise Men*) that, in order to explain it, we must suppose that the Limbourg masterpiece had become available to him after the death of Jean de Berry, when it belonged to Yolande of Aragon.

The Limbourgs so thoroughly dominated their period that it is not surprising to see them more imitated than many others. This imitation went as far as copying, pure and simple. The Saint Christopher painted on a separate folio now in Washington, D.C. (Figure XIII) is so like the one represented on a smaller scale in *The Belles Heures* (Figure XIV), that it has sometimes actually been attributed to the Limbourgs. A still more characteristic case, which this time concerns nearly an entire manuscript, occurred in *The Hours of Count Seilern*[15]—its painters obviously wished to make a kind of facsimile of *The Belles Heures*.

Unfortunately, the date of a specific manuscript cannot always be established with sufficient precision to allow us to determine in what direction transmissions of this type occurred. One is generally tempted to credit a superlative "master" with the responsibility for a figure, composition, or stylistic find in several visibly contemporary manuscripts, by virtue of the implicitly admissible principle that less accomplished and elaborate work could only have resulted from the degradation of a superior archetype. Yet sometimes the reverse occurred. The famous manuscript of the *Térence des Ducs* at the Bibliothèque de l'Arsenal (Plate 19) did not in any way serve as a model for the almost identical although slightly less magnificent *Térence* which is kept at the Bibliothèque Nationale,[16] as was supposed for sometime. On the contrary, it was for the latter manuscript that the original illustration program was developed, to be faithfully reproduced later in the Arsenal volume.

The Limbourgs themselves were not above re-employing the Frontispiece of a modest 1405 *Golden Legend*[17] for the painting of *The Heavenly Host* in *The Belles Heures*.[18] Their *Coronation of the Virgin* in *The Très Riches Heures* is keenly indebted to one that begins another *Golden Legend* and which can also be dated from the very first years of the fifteenth century (Figure XV).

Borrowings and re-utilizations of this type were innumerable. When an exhaustive and systematic inventory has been drawn up of all the many thousands of illuminations in public libraries and private collections throughout the world, there will undeniably be a quantity of others discovered which, until now, have escaped the investigations of researchers. Then, in a much more precise fashion, we shall be able to analyze and follow the entire progress of those multiple currents which gave the art of a precise period its specific characteristics.

An analysis reduced to a list of models and affiliations, however, would be insufficient. More subtle analogies can be discerned among the greater part of these works, some examples of which have been represented here. Different as these works may be from one another, they were immersed in the same atmosphere and express interpretations of similar forms of aesthetic sensibility.

A detailed examination of the technical processes that helped to give the

XIII   XIV

International Style its specific flavor is not possible within the limitations of a brief introduction. Very recently, the late-lamented Millard Meiss accomplished a masterful appraisal of a series of works of this period. His research has entirely revived the subject and made it possible to accurately identify all the new elements in the realms of composition, perspective and color that were injected into the venerable and traditional art of illumination at the beginning of the fifteenth century by the collective explorations of an entire generation. He also clarified, with the help of previous important contributions, that phenomenon of osmosis which spread from one corner of Western Europe to another in the form of the most unexpected convergences.

A precise example of this type of encounter is furnished by a rather exceptional method of composition used at the same time by the "Master of *The Rohan Hours*" and by a Hamburg painter known as "Meister Francke."[19] Both of them liked to create compositions in which background figures were immoderately large in proportion to those in the foreground. This was undoubtedly done to draw attention to the most important persons represented in the scene. Until proof to the contrary is furnished, we have no reason to suppose that, in painting his *Flight into Egypt* (Figure XVI) the "Master of *The Rohan Hours*" had been inspired by the retable that "Meister Francke" dedicated to the legend of

Saint Barbara (Figure XVII)—or vice-versa. An identical principle of composition is evident, however, in the two works.

The social ambiance of the times, a certain common sensibility, the atmosphere of refined elegance manifested by the principal courts, an accepted mode of attire, whose faithful representation was made mandatory in the secular scenes by the then-widespread taste for realism, contributed equally to the striking resemblances among the tiny figures who animate the vellum pages of so many manuscripts.

Thus, a certain drawing by a Rhenish master[20] will seem very similar to the figure of a seated young woman that appeared in the Calendar of *The Très Riches Heures* (Plate 26); or the painter of *The Hours of Marie de Gueldre* (Plate 34) will give his client a bearing and expression that would not be surprising in a figure painted by the Limbourgs.

The uncertainty that affects experts when they try to attribute a precise origin to a number of poorly identified works is a startling demonstration of that adherence to a common aesthetic code by artists living in very different regions.

The oft-cited resemblance between the first panel of *The Wilton Diptych*[21] and the page in *The Très Belles Heures of Notre Dame* which shows Jean de Berry among his patron saints (Plate 13), furnishes a fair example of this kind of problem. For quite some time the image of the barely adolescent Richard II of England (Figure XVIII) seemed most disconcerting; it apparently had to be dated from around the years 1375–1380 due to the age of the sovereign as portrayed. This conferred on the *Diptych* artist an extraordinary foresight, however, in exhibiting a style which would spread throughout Europe a generation later. Subsequently, Francis Wormald[22] has demonstrated with very convincing arguments that the painting must have been done around 1402, after the death of the sovereign, whose posthumous reknown it wished to assure. Nevertheless, Wormald could not, despite the precision of his inquiries, establish whether this was the work of a French or Flemish artist working in England, or an English artist who had thoroughly studied the technique of the continental masters.

Although it would be easy to prolong this kind of discussion, we will end it with one last example. This is furnished by a panel which everything urges us to date from the beginning of the fifteenth century[23] — everything, that is, except the image of the donor, substituted after 1452 for that of an unidentified personage. The figures of the Virgin and Child and the two saints (Figure XIX) belong to the initial state of the picture, and their style induced an art historian as informed as Panofsky to attribute them to a "Franco-Flemish" artist. More recently, however, the majority of specialists have generally agreed upon recognition of the hand of an artist from Lombardy, as betrayed by a certain stiffness in the drape of the Virgin's robe and the slightly vapid expression of

Cy commence le prologe de liure Jehan
du vignay de lordre de saint Jaques du
hault pas sur la legende dyce la quelle
il translata de latin en francois a lïnstance
et requeste de treshaute noble et puissante
dame ma dame de bourgoingne par la grace
de dieu royne de france

On seigneur saint geronne
dit ceste aucteure say tous
iours aucune chose que le
dyable ne te truisse oyseur
Et monseigneur saint augustin dist
on liure de loeuure des moynes que mil
home puissant de labourer ne doit estre
oyseur Pour la quelle chose quant Jos
pus fait et accompli le nombre des hysto
res du monde et translate de latin en

francois A la requeste de trespuissant
et noble dame ma dame Jehanne de
Bourgoigne par la grace de dieu Royne
de france Je fu tout esbahy a la quelle
euure fare Je me mettroye apres si tres
haulte et longue euure come Je auoye
faite par deuant Et pour ce que oysi
uete est tant blasmee que monseigneur
saint bernart dit quelle est mere des
truffes marrastre de vertus et celle q
trebuche les fors hommes en pechie
et fait estaindre vertus et nourir
orgueil et fait la vie valer en enfer
Et Jehan cassidore dit que la pensee de
celluy qui est oyseur ne pense a autre
chose que aux viandes pour son ventre
Et mons saint bernart dit en vne
epistre quant il nous commendra rene

30

XVI   XVII

the figures that one also finds in designs by Giovannino dei Grassi.

Such findings are perhaps less paradoxical than they might appear. They are, in effect, tantamount to recognizing that the works in question were all part of a strongly homogeneous artistic current. They could demonstrate, if need be, that proven multiple exchanges in this domain, within a very extensive geographical area where the same tastes and aesthetic conceptions prevailed, were effectuated in many diverse manners. Each center of production found itself, to some degree, in debt to all the others.

Born in France, in Italy, in Germany, in Austria, in Bohemia, in Catalonia, and in England, the forty images that will now speak for themselves will attest — even through their diversity — to the profound unity of a multi-faceted art. As Professor Philippe Verdier once stated, this art seems like a farewell to the Middle Ages at the very moment when it expressed the dream of permanence of a society already unknowingly being subjected to profound

XVIII

mutations. Just one more generation, two at the very most, and illumination, which had reached its zenith during the first quarter of the fifteenth century, will begin a downward path. Even the genius of a Fouquet, or the perfect craftsmanship of the last Italian illuminators will not be able to save it. Once illumination is thought of only as miniature easel painting, its obsolescence and state of decay will have become self-evident. And it would not be long afterward that the introduction of printing would deal this venerable art its final blow.

1. F. Avril, *Manuscript Painting at the Court of France*, New York and Paris 1978.
2. Bibliothèque Nationale, *La Librairie de Charles V*, Paris 1968. (Exhibition Catalogue).
3. See later "Selected Bibliography," pl. 24 and 25.
4. F. Avril, *op. cit.*
5. *Europäische Kunst um 1400 . . .*, Wien 1962. (Exhibition Catalogue).
6. F. Avril, *op. cit.*, p. 30, pl. 40 and Fig. XIII.
7. H. Martin, *La miniature française du XIII au XV siècle*, Paris, and Brussels 1923.
8. J. Porcher, *Jean Lebègue . . .*, Paris 1962.
9. F. Avril, *op. cit.*
10. See later "Selected Bibliography."
11. Paris, Bibliothèque Nationale, Ms. Lat. 9471, fol. 159.
12. See the various works of M. Meiss mentioned later in the "Selected Bibliography."
13. Paris, Bibliothèque Nationale, Ms. Lat. 9471, fol. 7.
14. H. Kreuter-Eggeman, *Das Skizzenbuch des "Jacques Daliwe,"* München 1964.
15. Private collection. See M. Meiss, *French Painting in the time of Jean de Berry–The Limbourgs and their Contemporaries*, New York 1974, p. 237 ff.
16. Paris, Bibliothèque Nationale, Ms. Lat. 7907A. See M. Thomas, "Une prétendue signature de peintre dans un manuscrit du debut de XV siècle," ds., *Bulletin de la Société nationale des Antiquaires de France*, (1958), p. 114 ff.
17. Paris, Bibliothèque Nationale, Fr. Ms. 414, fol. 1. See J. Porcher, *Les Belles Heures de Jean de France, duc de Berry*, Paris 1953, p. 12 and Fig. 2.
18. New York, the Cloisters, fol. 218.
19. Hamburger Kunsthalle, *Meister Francke und die Kunst um 1400*, Hamburg 1969 (Exhibition Catalogue).
20. *Europäische Kunst um 1400 . . .*, n. 265. pl. 113.
21. London, National Gallery.
22. F. Wormald, "The Wilton Diptych," ds. *Warburg Journal*, Vol. XVIII, (1954), pp. 191–203.
23. North Carolina Museum of Art. See Walters Art Gallery, *The Arts in Europe around 1400 — The International Style*, Baltimore 1962, (Exhibition Catalogue), n. 15 and pl. XXI.

XIX

SELECTED BIBLIOGRAPHY

So much has been written about Illuminated Manuscripts of the end of the fourteenth and the beginning of the fifteenth centuries that it would have been impossible to include all the books or articles mentioning any one of the manuscripts from which a page has been selected for reproduction in the present volume. Consequently, this is only a selection of the most recently published studies, most of which offer a complete bibliography of their subject. There are frequent references to Professor Millard Meiss's monumental works about the beginning of the fifteenth century; whenever appropriate, we briefly draw the reader's attention to their exhaustive bibliography. And reference to Millard Meiss's detailed information about specific manuscripts appears in bold face in the list of the pages mentioned.

Plate 1

M. Salmi, "La pittura e la miniatura gotica in Lombardia," ds., *Storia di Milano*, Milan 1955, t. V. p. 874.

P. Toesca, *La pittura e la miniatura nella Lombardia dai più antichi documenti alla metà del quattrocento*, second edition, Turin 1966, pp. 162–166, Figs. 330–334.

R. Lathuillière, *"Guiron Le Courtois", étude de la tradition manuscrite*, Geneva 1966.

M.L. Gengaro and L. Cogliati Arano, *Miniature Lombarde, codici miniati dall'VIII al XIV secolo*, Milan 1970, pp. 416–417 ff., Figs. 295–302.

Plate 2

L. Cogliati Arano, *The Medieval Health Handbook: Tacuinum Sanitatis*, translated and adapted from the Italian by Oscar Ratti and Adele Westbrook, New York 1976.

Plate 3

L. Castelfranchi Vegas, "Il libro d'ore Bodmer de Michelino da Besozzo e i rapporti tra miniatura francese e miniatura lombarda agli inizi del quattrocento," ds., *Etudes d'art français offertes à Charles Sterling*, Paris 1975.

R. Schilling, "Ein Gebetbuch des Michelino da Besozzo," ds., *Münchner Jahrbuch der bildenden Kunst*, 1957–58, p. 65 ff.

Plate 4

M. Meiss and E. W. Kirsch, *The Visconti Hours*, New York 1972, (Partial facsimile).

The same, *Les Heures Visconti*, translated from the American by F. Avril, Paris 1972 (French edition of the preceding work).

R. W. Scheller, *A Survey of Medieval Model Books*, Haarlem 1963.

Plate 5

P. Toesca, *"Le miniature dell'Elogio funebre* of G.G. Visconti," ds. *Rassegna d'Arte*, X, (1910), pp. 156–158.

P. Durrieu, "Michelino da Besozzo," ds., *Mem. de l'Acad. des Inscr. et belles lettres*, XXXVIII, (1911), pp. 365–393.

P. Toesca, work referred to under pl. 1.

P. D'Ancona, *La miniature italienne du Xe au XVIe s.*, Paris 1925, pp. 50–51, Fig. 60.

E. Pellegrin, *La bibliothèque des Visconti et des Sforza*, Paris 1925, 1938; and supplement, Paris 1969, pp. 33, 105.

L. Castelfranchi Vegas, work referred to under pl. 3.

Plate 6

"Twelve masterpieces of medieval and Renaissance book illumination. A Catalogue to the exhibition March 17–May 17, 1964," ds., *The Bull. of the Cleveland Museum of Art*, LI, March 1964, No. 8.

W. D. Wixom, "The Hours of Charles the Noble," ds., *The Bull. of the Cleveland Museum of Art*, LII, March 1965, pp. 50–83.

M. Meiss, *French Painting in the Time of Jean de Berry. The late XIVth century and the Patronage of the Duke*, London 1967, pp. 249–255, 323–324, Figs. 729–731, 734, 745, 749, 758, 761, 764, 772, 789, 804, 805, 809, 812, 813.

Plate 7

J. Porcher, "Le Bréviaire de Martin d'Aragon," ds., *France Illustration*, Special Christmas Number, (1950).

P. Bohigas, *La illustracion y la decoracion del libro manuscrito en Cataluña*, second edition, Barcelona 1960–1967.

Plate 8

P. Bohigas, work mentioned with reference to pl. 7, I, pp. 249–253, pl. 5.

Plate 9

Die goldene Bulle . . . vollständige Faksimile Ausgabe, W. Wolf, *Kommentar*, Graz 1977. (Integral facsimile)

G. Schmidt, "Malerei bis 1450. Tafelmalerei, Wandmalerei, Buchmalerei," ds., K.M. Swoboda, *Gothik in Böhmen*, Munich 1969, pp. 167–321.

F. Unterkircher, *Die datierten Handschriften der Oesterreichischen Nationalbibliothek bis zum Jahre 1400*, Vienna 1969, p. 19, pl. 268.

J. Krása, *Die Handschriften Königs Wenzels IV*, 1971, pp. 38–40, 217–222 ff., pl. 4.

Kaiser Karl IV, 1316–1378, Nürnberg Kaiserburg, Munich 1978, No. 145, (Exhibition Catalogue).

Plates 10–11

Ceske Umeni Goticki, 1350–1420, Prague 1970, No. 366 (Exhibition Catalogue) (See also bibliography for pl. 9).

Plate 12

P. Durrieu, "Les miniatures d'André Beauneveu," ds., *Le Manuscrit*, I, (1894), pp. 51–56, 83–95.

V. Leroquais, *Les psautiers manuscrits latins*, Mâcon, II, 1940–41, p. 144 ff.

M. Meiss, *The late XIVth century and the Patronage of the Duke*, London 1967, pp. 135–154, **331–334**, Figs. 51–82.

Plates 13–14

M. Meiss, *The late XIVth century and the Patronage of the Duke*, London 1967, pp. 194–228, **321–323**, Figs. 179–215.

Plate 15

M. Meiss, *The late XIVth century and the Patronage of the Duke*, London 1967, pp. 154–193, **334–337**, Figs. 83–176.

Plate 16

M. Meiss, *The Limbourgs and their Contemporaries*, New York 1974, pp. 7, 13, 23, 49, 98, **287–290**, 383, 418, Figs. 3, 46, 74, 200.

Bibliothèque Nationale, *Boccace en France*, Paris 1975, No. 94 (Exhibition Catalogue).

Plate 17

M. Meiss, *The late XIVth century and the Patronage of the Duke*, London 1967, p. **314**.

Plate 18

M. Meiss, *The Limbourgs and their Contemporaries*, New York 1974, pp. 8–41, **292–293**, Figs. 61, 62, 75, 76, 85, 87, 91, 102, 105, 106, 108, 122, 127, 133, 134, 138, 141, 146, 149.

Plate 19

M. Meiss, *The Limbourgs and their Contemporaries*, New York 1974, pp. 41–54, **336–339**, Figs. 63, 160, 161, 164, 176, 178, 182, 188, 193, 194, 199, 204, 210, 230.

Plate 20

M. Thomas, *Les grandes heures de Jean de France duc de Berry*, Paris 1971.

The Grandes Heures of Jean, Duke of Berry, translated by V. Benedict and B. Eisler, New York 1971, (Partial facsimile).

M. Meiss, *The late XIVth century and the patronage of the Duke*, London 1967, pp. 256–285, **332–334**, Figs. 216–244, 249, 251.

M. Meiss, *The Boucicaut Master*, London, New York 1968, pp. 12, 34, 68, 78, 95, 107, **125–126**, 129, 137, 147, 152, Figs. 61, 62.

M. Meiss, *The Limbourgs and their Contemporaries*, New York 1974, pp. 70, 94, 103, 106, 143, 155, 160, 180, 223, 234, 322, **365, 387**, 414, 416.

Plate 21

M. Meiss, *The late XIVth century and the Patronage of the Duke*, London 1967, pp. 227, 312, 363, 381, Fig. 683.

M. Meiss, *The Limbourgs and their Contemporaries*, New York 1974, pp. 44, 129, 213, 223, **343**, 348, 441, 474, 740, Figs. 167, 170.

Plate 22

Gaston Phoebus, *Livre de chasse*, G. Tilander ed., Karlshamn 1971.

Gaston Phoebus, *Le livre de la chasse, French ms. 616 in the Bibliothèque Nationale*. Introduction and commentaries by M. Thomas, F. Avril, and the Duc de Brissac. Translated into modern French by R. & A. Bossuat, Paris and Graz, 1976, (Complete facsimile).

Plate 23

E. Spencer, "The Master of the Duke of Bedford," ds., *Burlington Magazine*, CVII (1965), pp. 495–502, CVIII (1966), pp. 607–612.

D. H. Turner, *Illuminated Manuscripts in the Grenville Library*, London 1967, No. 58, pl. 14, (Exhibition Catalogue).

M. Meiss, *The de Lévis Hours and the Bedford Workshop*, New Haven 1972, pp. 13–15, 17–25, Figs. 20, 23, 31, 35, 38, 39, 45, 57–58.

M. Meiss, *The Limbourgs and their Contemporaries*, New York 1974, pp. 363–**364**, Fig. 777.

Plates 24 & 25:

J. Porcher, *Les Belles Heures de Jean de France duc de Berry*, Paris 1953, (Partial facsimile).

M. Meiss and E. Beatson, *The Belles Heures of Jean, Duke of Berry*, New York 1974, (Partial facsimile).

M. Meiss and E. Beatson, *Les Belles Heures du duc Jean de Berry*, translated by B. Bessard, Paris 1974.

M. Meiss, *The Limbourgs and their Contemporaries*, New York 1974, pp. 102–142, **331–336**, Fig. 329, etc.

Plates 26 & 27

The Très Riches Heures of Jean, Duke of Berry, Introduction and Captions by J. Longnon and R. Cazelles, Preface by M. Meiss, New York 1969.

Les Très Riches Heures du duc de Berry, Foreword by C. Samaran; Introduction and Captions by J. Longnon and R. Cazelles, Paris 1970.

M. Meiss, *The Limbourgs and their Contemporaries*, New York 1974, pp. 143–224, ff. **308–324**, Figs., 536–597, etc.

Plate 28

M. Meiss, *The Boucicaut Master*, London, New York 1968, pp. 7–22, **131–133**, Figs. 1–46, 48, 135.

Plate 29

M. Meiss, *The Boucicaut Master*, London, New York 1968, pp. 11, 24, 37, 68, 87, **124–125**, 145, 150, Figs. 67, 68, 70, 71.

Plate 30

M. Meiss, *The Boucicaut Master*, London, New York 1968, pp. 25, 34, 68, **87–88**, 124, 150, Figs. 69, 72–78.

B. Gagnebin, *L'enluminure de Charlemagne à François Ier. Les manuscrits â peintures de la Bibliothèque publique et universitaire de Genève*, Geneva 1976, pp. 87–90, No. 34, Figs. 69, 72–78.

Plate 31

M. Meiss, *The Boucicaut Master*, London, New York 1968, pp. 35, 38–40, 42, 68, 95, 116–122, Figs. 38, 44, 46, 80–100.

M. Meiss, *The Limbourgs and their Contemporaries*, New York 1974, pp. 367, 390, 417, 419.

Plates 32–33

Les Heures de Rohan, présentées et commentées by M. Meiss & M. Thomas, Paris 1973, (Partial facsimile).

The Rohan Master, A Book of Hours, Introduction by M. Meiss, Introduction and Commentaries by M. Thomas, translated by K.W. Carson, New York 1973.

M. Meiss, *The Limbourgs and their Contemporaries*, New York 1974, pp. 140, 256–277, 329, **352–353**, 358, Figs. 390, 829, 868–870, 872–877, 889, 898.

Plate 34

A. W. Byvanck, *De Middeleuwsche Boekillustratie in de Noordelijke Nederlanden*, Antwerp 1943, pp. 18–20.

Bibliothèque Royale Albert Ier. *La miniature hollandaise*, Brussels 1971, No. 8, p. 23, pl. 6, (Exhibition Catalogue).

Plate 35

H. Reinecke, *Lüneburger Buchmalereien um 1400*, Bonn 1937.

A. Boekler, *Deutsche Buchmalerei, II. Der Gotik*, Königstein 1959, pp. 8, 38.

Kunst um 1400, Vienna 1962, No. 204, pl. 146, (Exhibition Catalogue).

Charlemagne. Oeuvre. Rayonnement et Survivance, Aix-La Chapelle, 1965, No. 699, pl. 149. (Exhibition Catalogue).

Plate 36

A. Boeckler, *Deutsche Buchmalerei. II. Der Gotik*, Königstein 1959, p. 42.

B. Wohlgemuth, "Die Buchmalerei (Werkstatt der Grillinger-Bibel)," ds. *Spätgotik in Salzburg. Die Malerei*, Salzburg 1972, No. 237, p. 218.

C. Zügler, "Das Mondseer Urbar von 1416, ein Beitrag zur Frühphase der Werkstatt der Grillinger-Bibel," ds., *Öesterreichische Zeitschrift für Kunst und Denkmalpflege*, XXXI (1977), pp. 115–126.

Plate 37

The Sherborne Missal, Reproduction of full pages and details of ornaments, Introduction by J.A. Herbert, Oxford 1920, (Partial facsimile).

E. G. Millar, *English illuminated manuscripts, XIVth and XVth centuries*, 1928, pp. 32–34, 71–72, pl. 82–84.

La miniature anglaise aux XIVe et XVe siècles, translated by J. Buhot, Paris, and Brussels 1928, pp. 35–41, 75–76, pl. 82–84.

Bibliothèque Nationale, *Le livre anglais*, Paris 1951, No. 22, (Exhibition Catalogue).

British Museum, *English Book illustration 966–1846*, London 1965, p. 12.

Plate 38

E. G. Millar, work quoted for pl. 37, French edition, pp. 41–43, 76, pl. 85.

C. L. Kuhn, "Hermann Scheere," ds. *Art Bulletin*, XXII, (1940), Figs. 5–7.

M. Rickert, *The reconstructed Carmelite Missal*, London 1952, pp. 94–96, 138, 141, Plate LI.

E. Panofsky, *Early Netherlandish painting*, Cambridge 1953, pp. 116, 123, Figs. 173, 174.

British Museum, *English Book illustration 966–1846*, London 1965, pp. 12 and 16.

J. C. Skeat, *Illuminated manuscripts exhibited in the Grenville Library*, Edinburgh 1967, p. 17, pl. 8, (Exhibition Catalogue).

Plate 39

E. G. Millar, work quoted for pl. 37–38, French edition, pp. 44–45, 78, pl. 94.

Plate 40

E. G. Millar, work quoted for pl. 37, 38, 39, French edition, pp. 45, 79, pl. 95.

F. Saxl, R. Wittower, *British Art and the Mediterranean*, London, reprint 1969, pl. 35.

Bibliothèque Royale Albert Ier, *English Illuminated manuscripts*, Brussels 1973, No. 77, Color pl. 2. (Exhibition Catalogue).

LIST OF COLOR PLATES AND BLACK-AND-WHITE FIGURES

Plates and Commentaries

PLATE 1

The Romance of Guiron Le Courtois
fol. 55   *A Tournament*

The original text of this beautiful, although extremely fragmentary, manuscript of a courtly novel was composed between 1215 and 1230, and extensively rewritten later, with numerous additions. Its decoration was most probably executed in Lombardy during the last quarter of the fourteenth century, but it is not known for whom it was originally intended. The 110 pages that have come down to us are illustrated with large, borderless paintings, usually placed at the bottom of the page. They represent chivalric or courtly battle scenes, tournaments, banquets, gallant encounters, and so forth.

In this manuscript, the illustrations consist of watercolor sketches rather than paintings. Their light, subtly blended colors permit full appreciation of the refinement and surety of line. The use of *grisaille* and monochrome was also favored by certain illustrators of this *Guiron*.

Toesca linked the present volume to the *Lancelot* manuscript from the Library of the Dukes of Milan (Paris, Bibl. Nat. Fr. Ms. 343), thinking that it may have been of Lombard origin. More recently, other specialists in Italian illumination have detected certain Venetian characteristics in the work. (Existing relationships between Lombardy and Venice at the end of the fourteenth century might actually be an additional argument in favor of this theory.)

The hand of one of the illustrators of this manuscript seems, moreover, to reappear in a copy of the *Valerius Maximus* in Bologna (Bibl. Univ. Ms. 2463), and all specialists agree that the *Guiron* dates from the last years of the fourteenth century.

The page reproduced here illustrates a tournament. Two groups of cavaliers are engaged in a vigorous encounter before the eyes of a mainly feminine audience; from wooden stands decorated with draperies the spectators follow the competition with keen interest.

The organization of the composition follows a rigorous axial symmetry which is further stressed by the disposition of the stands.

veu le bon chr̄ sanz peor. Q̄ue ou venuz est sanz faille. ci set il de moi nulle nouell. sur oil si me oselt der. il reconuit maintenant ce ge ge disoie de uos. ce me dist un de sa c̄pagnie or me di fet li rois q̄l gent a il en sa c̄pagnie. S̄ire il a ueil. oylande. et mis. bl̄y. et miser G. et d̄eus autres c̄paiḡnos. H̄a fer li rois oxely. puis q̄l a cels auer lui li rois artus i est sanz faille. P̄l me poise de mō seignor q̄ entre moi portera armes a ceste asemblee. q̄ ne fait de touz les autres. bīe puet dire le bō chr̄ sāz peor q̄l a uoo beze chr̄ aueer lui. lors s̄en uait li roi pelinor et li dit tout cest afaire. et il responde sur se der me oselt il me poise de ce qe li rois ua entre nos. mes puis qe nos entrez en cestui fait. il est mestier qe nos trauaillō en sit qe nos en issōm a henor:.

E̅ t sint pu̅le li roi oxely. et li roi pelinor de lōr s̄apareil. li autres chr̄ q̄ par le chastil estoient si font grāt ioie a se solacet durent. A trei a qe il targe mout qe la hore. q̄ le roi soit uenuz q̄l fussēt en celle besoiḡe. lor armes sōt ap̄ reliees et les chenax. mout se trauaille chac̄us en diuit foi dit forbir ses armes. et cil ki q̄ cheual a et bō et bel. il s̄en tiēt auḡs bī paies. li roi de nobelande fuit demād. qant chr̄ poroit estre de sa partie. Et li augāt dict q̄l poront bien estre dus q̄ a. D̄. de sa p̄tie. li roi en est liez. et de ce tes nouell se uait il mout fort sfortāt. celle nuit soit si ḡnt leete n si ḡnt feste. en cest chastel. qe len ni oist d̄eu tonoit. la ville bruit tote de ioie. i eist sōt tuit en pouere a riche. A lendemai gant il aiorne li chr̄ q̄ en pens esloient de porter armes

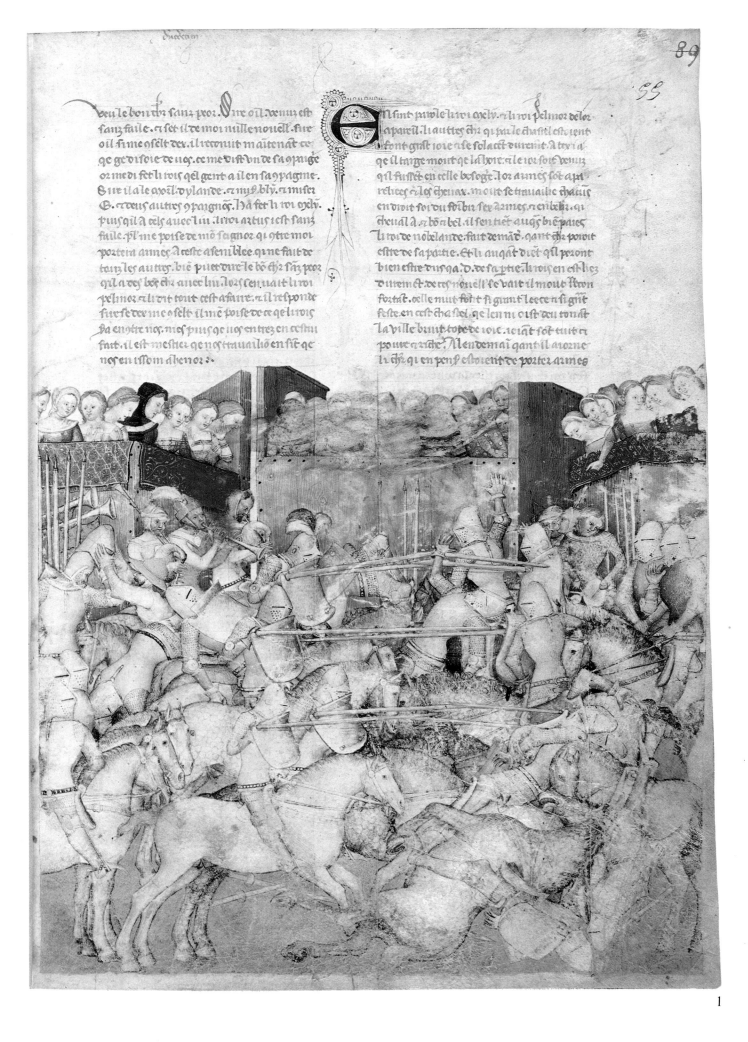

1

PLATE 2

THE TACUINUM SANITATIS
fol. 25   *Orgeat (Aqua Ordei)*

The medical and pharmacological treatise written by the Arab Ibn Botlân during the middle of the tenth century was later translated into Latin under conditions that have remained rather obscure. It is known that one translation was done between 1254 and 1266 at the court of King Manfred of Sicily, but others may have already existed at that time. The various versions of the work, which appeared in increasing number during the fourteenth and fifteenth centuries, especially in Italy, are called *Tacuina Sanitatis*. The first of these two words, derived from the Arabic, means more or less: "table" or "catalogue"; the second indicates the type of information assembled therein, in this case ideas and advice concerning health and well-being.

A copy, from which a page has been reproduced here, belonged to a Princess of the Milanese Visconti family, wife of Leopold III of Hapsburg, Duke of Austria. The book's illustration has been attributed to illuminators who came from either Verona or Lombardy, but the second hypothesis is more likely. The date of the book's execution lies, of necessity, between the marriage of Verde Visconti to Leopold, in 1365, and the Princess's death in 1405, but it seems closer to the later date.

The colors used by the artist—or artists—who decorated the manuscript, and especially the use of *grisaille*, show a French influence frequently found in Lombard manuscripts of the same era (Plate 5). Toesca took the illustration to be the work of Giovannino and Salomone dei Grassi.

The few lines of text on the lower part of the page deal with the virtues and characteristics of *orgeat*, a barley decoction resembling "barley water." We learn that this beverage is of a "cold and dry" nature. The best *orgeat* is obtained by prolonged boiling, which softens it. It is excellent for heartburn, but harmful for sufferers of "coldness in the intestines" — fortunately this negative aspect can be overcome by adding sugar to the beverage!

Aqua ordei.

y natnre. t. a. f. m. 2. melior ecci. coplete orta leius.
Juuamentum. epati calido. nocumentum. uiscerib9
frigidis. remotio nocumenti. cu zuchato rosaceo.

52

2

3

PLATE 3

THE BODMER HOURS
fol. 75   *Saint Luke*

This volume is the only known fragment of a most luxurious Book of Hours—the kind the Viscontis used to order from the best artists in Lombardy at the end of the fourteenth and the beginning of the fifteenth centuries. We do not know for whom it was executed, or under what circumstances, and its history remained obscure until Professor Otto Pächt was able to study it for the first time. At that point the volume was in Switzerland and belonged to Martin Bodmer's renowned collection. Later it was acquired by the Pierpont Morgan Library in New York.

Otto Pächt recognized in this manuscript the work of the great Michelino da Besozzo, a painter whom his contemporary, Alcherius, considered "the most excellent of all the painters in the world."

The Bodmer Hours are most remarkable for their borders. The decorative style adopted by Michelino shows an extraordinary spirit of innovation. The tri-lobed foliage that had been the fashion in France for so long was replaced here, for the first time, by flora of elegant variety: violets, bearbine, columbine, periwinkle, lilies, and cyclamens, copied from nature with a keen sense of observation. The artist's botanical exactitude reminds us of the illustrators of the *Tacuina Sanitatis* (Plate 2), but his work has a freshness and delicacy of color which the others did not attain. He has dedicated each page to a different flower, which occasionally reappears in the background of the painting which it frames—its color always in perfect harmony with the painting.

It is difficult to date this volume. In view of the richness and maturity of its style, Mrs. Castelfranchi Vegas recently, and most convincingly, has proposed that *The Bodmer Hours* could hardly be prior to 1405–1410, since Michelino's activity as an illuminator occurred between 1395 and 1415. Although a French influence can be detected in Michelino's illuminations, the influence of his border innovations began crossing the Alps in the opposite direction from 1420 onward. This interaction is an additional justification for the adjective "International" so aptly applied to the style of the years 1390 to 1430.

In the present reproduction we see that Michelino has placed Saint Luke in the setting of a painter's workshop, as a reminder that he is the Patron Saint of that profession; the Saint is putting the finishing touches to a wooden panel representing the Virgin. His artist's implements have been painted with an obvious desire for realism, which does, however, lack the precision of the Dutch illuminators who illustrated Boccaccio (Plate 16). The background of flowers and the presence of the calf (the symbol of Saint Luke) by his side, link this illumination to a relatively archaic tradition.

4

PLATE 4

THE VISCONTI HOURS
fol. 46   *The Creation of Eve*

The history of *The Visconti Hours* comprises several episodes. Its "wonderful extravagance" dazzled Millard Meiss when he first leafed through it in 1947, after Baron Finaly had donated it to the Uffizi Museum in Florence.

This Book of Hours had been ordered by Giangaleazzo Visconti (1351–1402) shortly before his accession to the Duchy of Milan in 1395. In addition to being a man of letters, a humanist, and a great lover of the arts, he was a passionate huntsman with, moreover, a keen interest in the natural sciences. This taste, unusual for his time, found expression in the decorative subjects chosen by the artists whom he entrusted with the illustration of this manuscript. It was to be sumptuous enough to compete with those of his brother-in-law, the Duke de Berry.

Initially, Giovannino dei Grassi and his collaborators had been chosen to decorate the manuscript, after a certain "Frater Amadeus" had finished copying the text. Giovannino, who also worked as a sculptor and *capomaestro* at the Milan Cathedral, died in 1398, before he could complete *The Visconti Hours*. Giangaleazzo died shortly afterward, and it was not before 1430 (?) that the Duke Filippo-Maria decided to have work resumed on the volume. For this purpose he contacted Belbello da Pavia, who was later to illustrate *The Este Bible* and work for the Gonzaga family of Mantua. When completed, the two parts of *The Visconti Hours* were bound in separate volumes which had different fates until their recent and final reunion at The National Library in Florence.

The page reproduced here belongs to The Hours of the Virgin (Compline) and is the work of Belbello. In the large *C* which begins the invocation *"Converte nos Deus . . . ,"* God the Father's torso stands out against a golden background as He causes a plump blonde Eve to emerge from Adam's sleeping body. A variety of fauna animates the margins. Fabulous beasts such as a griffin and a unicorn are placed next to animals visibly copied from nature, such as the cheetah, whose collar clearly indicates that it belonged to some illustrious menagerie. The same animal recurs almost identically in an album of sketches attributed to Giovannino dei Grassi, kept today at Bergamo, and in the Missal executed for Giangaleazzo in 1395. The whole page is, in fact, reminiscent of Giovannino. The steep rocks which line the landscape also suggest a somewhat archaic inspiration, and it is not impossible that the margins of this page were at least sketched during the initial illustration campaign. In the upper margin we note escutcheons held aloft by flights of angels bearing the Visconti arms: the famous *biscia*, a terrifying snake devouring a child.

PLATE 5

PIETRO DE CASTELLETTO: GIANGALEAZZO VISCONTI'S FUNERAL EULOGY
fol. 1   *The Apotheosis of Giangaleazzo Visconti*

This manuscript belonged to the Library of the Dukes of Milan in Pavia before it became part of the collections of Louis XII of France at the end of the fifteenth century.

It contains two texts by the same author, both written in praise of Giangaleazzo Visconti, Duke of Milan, who died in 1402. The first is a eulogy that Pietro de Castelletto, Hermit of Saint Augustine, recited publicly in Milan at the Duke's funeral on October 2. The other is the genealogy of the Dukes of Milan by the same author. It is illustrated by a series of portraits in *grisaille* and traces the ducal lineage back to Anchises and Aeneas, and forward to Giangaleazzo's son.

The frontispiece of the funeral eulogy reproduced on the opposite page represents Giangaleazzo in Paradise, being crowned by the Infant Jesus, whom the Virgin is holding in her lap. Around them, a heavenly court composed of angels and women symbolizing the virtues watches the scene.

Representing an attempt at flattery that bordered on sacrilege, the composition was visibly inspired by the traditional iconography of the Coronation of the Virgin, a subject often treated in illuminations of that period.

The large initial which begins the text is filled with a group of clerical personages mourning the departed; its borders are embellished with a frieze of characters.

The Visconti emblem (a radiant sun bearing a dove) appears in the upper and lower margins of the page which is framed by a light plant border in which quadrilobes with the Visconti escutcheon alternate with busts of the Prophets, identifiable by the text written on the phylacteries beneath each bust.

At the beginning of the twentieth century, Toesca, followed by Zappa and by Count Durrieu, attributed the decoration of the manuscript to the Lombard painter Michelino da Besozzo, who worked in Pavia and Milan between 1388 and 1415, and signed "The Mystical Marriage of Saint Catherine" which is in the Siena Picture Gallery. Later, d'Ancona justly pointed out that the influence of the French style upon Lombard illumination at the end of the fourteenth and the beginning of the fifteenth centuries was particularly strong in the work of Michelino, thus bringing new strength to his predecessors' hypothesis.

Sermo factus et recitatus per Magistrum petrum de Castelleto, ordinis heremitarum sancti Augustini, in exequiis quondam illustrissimi domini Ducis Mediolani, papie virtutium comitis, Bononie, Pisarum, Senarum ac perusii domini Johannis Galeaz, MCCCCII, XX octobris Mediolani in eius palatio hora vigesima prima.

Eu principes et Magistratus, heu presules, vrin gens Senatus, heu nobiles et ciuium apparatus quid ad egros solandos egri or missus sum, qd crudo uulneri cicatricem superducere conor, quid tanto uirtutum splendore hic adunato inscius et ignarus coram blacterare psumo, hec me arcent ne loquar, hec mutum efficiunt. Sed prepotentissimi Illustrissimi ac Magnificentissimi Ducis nostri comune dispendium urget ne sileam, coarctat ut eius laudes toti mundo fulgentes vobis depromam, quod in tam perfacile foret qp noctue solis radios clara luce intueri. dicam tamen no ex fiducia ingenij at diuino perfusus numine, qd pro modulo mee paruitatis sufficiet, proponens vestris maiestatibus ad honorem nostri ducis uerbum quod scribitur primi macha beorum, xij, in fine capituli. posuit eum ducem virtutum uniuersarum.

PLATE 6

THE HOURS OF CHARLES THE NOBLE
p. 191   *The Coronation of the Virgin*

Charles III, King of Navarre, Count d'Évreux, and Duke de Nemours (1361–1425), was known as Charles "The Noble." During the course of his reign he visited Paris a number of times and it was there, probably shortly after 1495, that he acquired this exceptionally beautiful Parisian Book of Hours. The page reproduced here is a particularly tangible example of the "International" character of the new style that was evolving at the time.

The illustration of the book was executed by artists from widely differing backgrounds. If this resulted in a certain disparity, the unexpected blending of their different approaches within the same volume was, nonetheless, typical of the eclectic taste of the period.

The illuminator who illustrated most of the volume, and therefore is usually assumed to have been the head of the artistic team, was decidedly Italian. Everything in his technique demonstrates this, especially the marginal illustrations, with *putti* or *ignudi* playing among large acanthi in a rain of gold dots.

According to certain opinions, the Italian inscription found in another page on a book held by a hybrid could be the signature of the artist, whose name should read "Zebo da Firenze," but this interpretation is doubtful. It seems wiser to continue calling this particular painter the "Brussels Initials Master," a name given him by Millard Meiss, as a reminder that, before 1402, he had had a hand in the illustration of the *Très Belles Heures de Notre Dame*, now belonging to the Belgian Royal Library (Plate 13).

The style of this painter, as well as that of his assistants, is reminiscent of the artistic milieu of Bologna or Padua, and is also recognizable in some ten manuscripts that were illustrated between 1390 and 1410, two of which, at least, were intended for Italian patrons. It is interesting to note how he managed to incorporate certain iconographic themes of Northern origin into *The Hours of Charles the Noble*. He treats these subjects in a manner that is not strictly Italian, even though his "Italianisms" are quite obvious.

The five paintings which illustrate the various stages of the Passion of Christ are, on the contrary, the work of an artist who sought his inspiration and his models in Flemish art, and whom Millard Meiss has called the "Egerton Master."

Around 1405, the principal illuminator of *The Hours of Charles the Noble* introduced Italian decorative and architectural motifs into the artistic milieu of France, where the Limbourgs were then learning their craft. Thus, he played quite an important part in the development of the so-called International Style, which aimed mainly at the assimilation and harmonious fusion of heterogenous pictorial traditions.

PLATE 7

THE BREVIARY OF MARTIN OF ARAGON
fol. 145   *The Adoration of the Magi*

Martin V, known as "The Elder," was the last King of the Catalan dynasty to rule over Aragon — from 1395 (when he succeeded his brother John I) to his death in 1410.

Fortunately we have the letters he wrote to the Abbot of Poblet (a Cistercian Abbey of Catalonia, where the Kings of Aragon were buried), concerning the sumptuous Breviary he had ordered. These letters reveal both the liturgical concerns of this monarch who was known for his piety, and the conditions under which the manuscript was copied and decorated. On February 17, 1398, Martin stressed the exceptional length of the "lessons" he wanted for his Breviary; shortly thereafter he informed the Abbot that he had dispatched a shipment of skins of the finest quality to him. We can deduce from this correspondence that the illuminations of the volume were far from finished in 1403, because at that point the King asked the Abbot to look for an illuminator who could help execute the "stories" that were to decorate the volume. Moreover, he promised to send his personal illuminator to Poblet at a later date, to give the work a finishing touch. This particular detail demonstrates once again the collective character of most of these large-scale artistic projects, and makes us realize that it is often difficult, under these conditions, to pinpoint the exact contribution of each collaborator.

It is possible that a painter from Valencia by the name of Domingo Crespi worked on the book, in collaboration with a certain Peire Soler, but this remains hypothetical.

Close commercial and artistic ties existed at that time between Catalonia and Italy —to cite one example: the "San Marco Master," the creator of the Manrese Triptych, was visibly influenced by the Italian painters of the late fourteenth century. It is not surprising, therefore, that the vivid, boldly contrasting colors used by the painters of the Breviary should recall those favored by Italian illuminators of the same period, especially those who worked on *The Visconti Hours* (Plate 4). The gold dots studding the margins of the Breviary, as well as the accompanying floral motifs, are also of Italian origin.

Nevertheless, it must be stressed that the iconography of the Calendar — which was directly inspired by the style of Jean Pucelle that appeared around 1320, and was brought back into fashion toward the very end of the fourteenth century by Jean de Berry's painters—also points to French influences in this manuscript. In any case, *The Breviary of Martin of Aragon* is an excellent example of the convergent tendencies which gave early fifteenth-century illumination its truly "International" character.

PLATE 8

The Missal of Saint Eulalia
fol. 7   *The Last Judgment*

It is rather unusual to have as much precise knowledge about the history of a manuscript as is the case for this beautiful Catalan Missal. It was donated to the Barcelona Cathedral by Juan Ermengol, Abbot of San Cugat del Valle, and confidant to King Martin the Elder, after his appointment as Bishop of Barcelona in September 1398. Moreover, a document dated 1403 indicates that on March 8 of that year, Bishop Ermengol charged an illuminator by the name of Rafael Destorrents with the illustration of a Missal which that artist completed in September—and for which he was paid the sum of 11 pounds. This is unquestionably the same Missal that the Bishop donated to his church and that contains the page reproduced here.

Rafael Destorrents must have been born around 1375, because a document dated May 22, 1391, states that he was sixteen years old at that time. In October 1395, another document refers to him as an illuminator. It is known that he eventually received holy orders and belonged to the Barcelona clergy.

The Missal which he adorned with eighteen illuminated initials, and a page consecrated to *The Last Judgment* which immediately follows the Calendar, mentions the days of many Catalan saints, especially that of Saint Eulalia of Merida, to whom the Missal owes its name.

The style of the decoration shows a distinct kinship with *The Breviary of Martin of Aragon* (Plate 7), which was produced at about the same time. The artistic importance of the Missal is probably even greater than that of the Breviary, although its decoration is less lavish. Bohigas considers it "an unequalled work, the acme of the school which flourished in Catalonia and in Valencia at the end of the fourteenth and at the beginning of the fifteenth century."

Despite its modest reduction to a marginal border role, this *Last Judgment* is skillfully organized on three levels. At the bottom, under the slabs of a kind of underground crypt, the damned in hell suffer torments meted out to them by demons that look, in some instances, like forerunners of those of Hieronymus Bosch. In the lateral margins, the dead rise from their tombs, called forth by the trumpets of angels. In the upper border, Christ in glory receives and blesses the chosen, surrounded by his heavenly court.

Dniica .î. aduetus to offin
do te leuaui aîaz meaz. do
nis in te confido nó eru
bescaz . neqʒ irrideat me inimi
ci mei et ei uniii qui te expec
tant nó ȝfundetur. Vrias tu
as dñe demostra m. p Et se
mitas tuas edoce me. Slia
Et nota qʒ non dicatur
Slia inexcelsis deo. Ozo
Excita dñe ptentia tu
am et ueni . ut ab in
minetibʒ ptctoz nroz pi
culis . te inceamur . p tege
te eripi . te libante salua
ri. Vl iii. le ad romanos.

Frs . Saētes qʒ hoza ē
lia nos te sopno sur
gere. Nūc . at . ppr. ē nra sa
lus. qʒ cū credidimʒ. Por
pcessit dies . at . appiquauit
Abiciam ȝ opa tenebraz
et iduamur arma lucas sic
ut idie honeste ambulem?
Nó i comessacdibʒ . et ebri
etatibʒ. Nó in cubilibʒ . et
impudiciaȝs . Nó i contentio
ne . z emulacione. Set in
duimini . dñz nrz ihz xpz.
Et Vniii q te expectat nó ȝ
fundetur dñe. Vrias tuas dñe
notas fac m z semitas tuas edo

PLATE 9

THE GOLDEN BULL OF EMPEROR CHARLES IV
fol. 1.   *Christ in Majesty — King Wenceslas and the Bathers*

The Emperor Charles IV was the maternal uncle of Charles V, King of France. In 1355 – 1356, at the Diets of Nuremberg and Metz, he promulgated a document regulating the election procedures of the Emperors of Germany. The term "Golden Bull," given to this document, recalls the particular nature of the seal traditionally affixed to such a document, in order to stress its official importance.

A copy of the "Golden Bull," whose first page is reproduced here, was transcribed and decorated in 1400—as indicated in its colophon (f. 460)—at the order of Wenceslas, the son of Charles IV. He bore the double title of King of the Romans and King of Bohemia, but in July 1400 the Diet denied him the office of Emperor.

Wenceslas was a great lover of art and books. He contributed to the flowering of the arts within the confines of his realm, and Bohemia experienced what has been called "the golden age" of its painting during his reign.

The first page of the "Golden Bull" is an excellent example of the Bohemian "beautiful style" of illumination; it is deeply marked by Italian influences and occupies an important position in the International art of the beginning of the fifteenth century. In the right-hand column, illustrating the Prayer to the Creator which opens the text of the Bull, Christ in Majesty has been represented between two angels. The softness of the faces, the balanced composition, and the tonalities of the painting are typical of Bohemian art.

The particularly careful execution of the borders differs from that in manuscripts previously executed for Wenceslas. The birds perched on large plant shoots exemplify a preoccupation with naturalism which can also be found in certain contemporary "pattern books," notably that of Giovannino dei Grassi.

In the lower margin, the artist has humorously portrayed Wenceslas himself, as though caged within the bars of his initial *W.* Posed like David peeping at the bathing Bathsheba, the King takes visible delight in watching a group of more or less nude women bathers. In the upper left margin, a "savage" presents an escutcheon of the arms of Bohemia. In the center of the upper margin we recognize the imperial eagle, under a helmet with a plumed crest, an allusion to Wenceslas's candidature to the title that was soon to be denied him. The initial *O* in the left column is decorated with a "love knot," an emblem that is found frequently in manuscripts decorated for Wenceslas (Plate 10).

 N anegenge schepfte got hmel
vnd erde. Die erde was aber vnuuer
vnd lere vnd vinsternuffe warn
auf der gestalt der abegrund vn
gotes geift wart gefurt auf den
waffern. vnd got spuache. Es
werde ein liecht vnd es wart ein
liecht. vnd got sach das liecht
das es gut was vnd schid das
liecht von der vinsternuffe. vnd
nante das liecht tack vnd die vi
sternuffe nacht. vnd wart ge
macht abent vnd morgen ein
tag. vnd got sprach. Es werde
ein veftenunge in der mitte der
waffer vnd teilte die waffer vo
den waffern. Vnd got machte
ein firmament. vnd schied die
waffer die do waren vnder dem
firmament von den die do wa
ren auf dem firmament. vnd
es geschach also. Vnd got nan
te das firmament himel. vnd
wart gemacht abent vnd mor
gen der ander tag. Got vnser
sprach. Die waffer die vnder dem
himel fint sammen sich an ein
ftat vnd erscheine die trucken
vnd es geschach also. vn got
nante die trucken erde vnd die
sammenunge der waffer nante
her die mer. vnd got sach das
es gut was. Vnd sprach. Ge
bere die erde grunende wurtze
vnd machende samen. Vnd
ein opfeltragendes holtz vnd

PLATE 10

The Bible of King Wenceslas
Vol. I fol. 2   *The Creation*

Among the seven or eight manuscripts which today are definitely known to have belonged to the collection of King Wenceslas of Bohemia, a large German Bible in six volumes undisputably deserves first place. It was executed for him around 1390 or shortly thereafter.

As in the previously mentioned copy of the "Golden Bull" (Plate 9), artists who worked on the decoration of this Bible frequently alluded to the personality of the great lover of books who was also their monarch.

In the margins of the page reproduced here appear the arms of the Empire and of the Kingdom of Bohemia; another escutcheon—half obliterated—probably bore the arms of Bavaria, in memory of the King's first spouse, Joan of Bavaria. The "love knots," the halcyon, the other birds, the bathing woman (who, according to certain opinions, resembles Queen Sophia, Wenceslas's second wife), and the large initial *E*, crowned with a miter, from which protrudes the King's jester, represent as many marks of ownership as can be found in all the other manuscripts in the monarch's possession.

An undertaking as extensive as the decoration of this immense Bible necessarily required the collaboration of several artists. Krasa has attributed the 249 illustrations in the first volume to three different masters. According to him, its first illumination, which is traditionally dedicated to the theme of the Creation, was the work of the "Willehalm Master," so named because, in 1387, he illustrated a novel by that title for Wenceslas. Other scholars have refrained from taking a decisive stand on this attribution, and prefer to call the author of this composition "The Master of the Seven Days."

According to custom, each of these medallions depicted a day of the Creation as reported in Genesis. However, the present series shows certain intriguing divergences from the sacred text. If it had remained faithful to the text (Gen. 1: 20–23, 24–25), the fifth medallion, which follows the one representing the Creation of the birds and the fish, should actually have preceded it.

The scenes of the Creation are framed by faces of the Apostles (some of them, such as Saint Peter, Saint Paul, and Saint John, are readily identifiable), and of the Prophets. This parallelism of Apostles and Prophets is common in medieval iconography.

PLATE 11

THE BIBLE OF KING WENCESLAS
Vol. II fol. 145   *The Death of Jezebel*

The second volume of the Bible, the frontispiece of which is reproduced on the preceding Plate, contains the Books of *Judges, Ruth,* and *Kings.* The last of these has been interrupted by the modern rebinding of the manuscript, which did not respect the original divisions.

The illustration consists of 233 small paintings and six decorated initials at the beginning of each Book. As in the preceding volume, the illustration represents the collective enterprise of several artists. Scholars are not in complete agreement as to their number: some have distinguished nine, others only five different illuminators.

At any rate, we do know the name of two of the artists. The signature "Frana, illuminator," which appears on several works, has been rather convincingly identified as being that of a court illuminator named Franois, whose work began to appear on several documents from 1397 onward. The other artist signed his name in two places in the manuscript, but no other trace has been found of the work of this "N. Kuthner."

The folio reproduced here cannot be attributed to either of these two artists. It depicts the Death of Jezebel, the widow of King Ahab (IV Reg. IX, 31–37). Considered the incarnation of evil, Jezebel was cursed by the Lord. She was thrown from a window, and the dogs fought over her dead body. In the seventeenth century, Racine incorporated this dramatic episode into his *Athalie.* It shows to what extent the human imagination has been struck by the horrible, if deserved, fate of this unworthy Queen.

In this instance, the episode has been treated with great simplicity. It is strange that no architecture is shown in the background of the painting, although the biblical text specifies that Jezebel was thrown down from the top of a building (the defenestration theme had been frequently used by illuminators since the fourteenth century, especially in the workshops which followed Pucelle's tradition).

Beyond several trees which break the monotony of a strictly conventional rock landscape, an ominously black background is vaguely illuminated by large golden *rinceaux.* Bohemian illuminators were extremely fond of this type of background, which was occasionally imitated by their Parisian colleagues, especially in a copy of Gaston Phébus's *Livre de la Chasse,* a folio of which has been reproduced in this book (Plate 22).

lic wil en laten vber vlch
plses vnd wil abe howen
deine hinderisten vnd wil

vozterben von achaben den
seichenden an die want vñ
den vozslosnen in yschahel
vnd wil geben dein haus

effundam de
spiritu meo
super omne
carnem.

ur tous le
donray de
mon ef
prit.

12

PLATE 12

THE PSALTER OF JEAN DE BERRY
fol. 19   *The Prophet Joel*

The inventory of Jean de Berry's books, compiled in 1402, listed a Psalter in Latin and French, which contained "several stories" (meaning paintings) by André Beauneveu. It is more than probable that *The Psalter of Jean de Berry*, a folio of which is reproduced here, is the Psalter listed in the inventory. We also have the relatively rare good fortune to be almost certain of the name of the artist who executed the twenty-four large paintings which precede the Psalter proper. The rest of the illustrations were done by other illuminators who worked in a totally different spirit.

André Beauneveu began his career in Valenciennes. From about 1372 to 1381 he worked for Louis de Male, Count of Flanders, before entering the service of Jean de Berry, around 1384. He was foremost a sculptor, and when he took part in the decoration of the Psalter commissioned by his master, he visibly fell back on his previous experience, when he used to "cut images" in three dimensions.

His contribution to the Psalter consisted of large, full-page figures, each representing one of the Apostles, faced, on their opposite pages, by twelve Prophets of the Old Testament. They can be recognized by a quotation from the Bible, copied under the painting.

The linking of Prophets and Apostles is not an iconographic innovation, and the excerpts of text which accompany the paintings have varied little since the end of the thirteenth century. Since there are more Prophets than Apostles, there may have been some hesitation as to the choice of Prophets to be juxtaposed with the twelve Apostles. The subject appears for the first time in a manuscript of the *Verger de soulas*, before reappearing in *Queen Mary's Psalter*, the *Belleville Breviary*, and a number of later manuscripts which followed the iconographic tradition of Pucelle's calendars. It is certainly not mere coincidence that Beauneveu treated his majestic figures in extremely light tones; his skillful use of monochrome gradation suggests the idea of relief far better than a contrast of colors. The tonalities of the background were utterly new; Prophets and Apostles sit on thrones of great architectural elegance, with a tessellated background, which further accentuates the sculptural aspect of the figures.

Under the painting, a sentence from the prophecies of Joel has been inscribed, both in Latin and in French: "I will pour out my spirit upon all flesh. . ." (Joel 1:28).

13

PLATE 13

THE TRÈS BELLES HEURES OF NOTRE DAME
p. 10   *Jean de Berry between his Patron Saints John and Andrew*

The 1402 inventory lists among Jean de Berry's manuscripts a *Très Belles Heures* richly illuminated and illustrated by the hand of "Jacquemart de Odin." It further specifies that the owner later gave this manuscript to Jean sans Peur, Duke of Burgundy.

Despite a few gaps in its further history, this *Très Belles Heures* can be convincingly identified as the manuscript in two volumes presently at the Royal Library in Brussels.

This Book of Hours opens most unusually with two large paintings forming a diptych. Originally, they were not an integral part of the manuscript, and their framing differs from that of paintings which appear later. The verso of the first folio of this diptych has been reproduced here: it shows the Duke de Berry in prayer, in the company of, and as though morally supported by, his Patron Saints John the Baptist and Andrew—readily recognizable by their traditional attributes: the slanted Cross for Saint Andrew and the Easter Lamb for Saint John.

The attitudes of the figures may seem somewhat strange if the page is considered separately, but the wing of the diptych facing this page provides the explanation, since it represents the Virgin and the Divine Child, and it is to them that the two Saints are presenting and recommending their namesake.

The scale of the figures on these two pages and their arrangement, as well as the treatment of the draperies and faces, recall panel paintings rather than illuminations. They contrast sharply with the manuscript, which is the work of several artists and cannot be attributed to Jacquemart de Hesdin, despite the mention in the inventory quoted above. That particular artist's style is totally different. However, an earlier theory set forth by Leopold Delisle, which attributed the diptych to André Beauneveu, the creator of the large figures of Prophets and Apostles in the front of the *Psalter of Jean de Berry* (Plate 12), still appears extremely likely. Millard Meiss dated these two paintings around 1390, and saw them as the successful assimilation by a Northern artist of Italian traditions, especially those expressed by Simone Martini. In a way, these paintings also recall the Wilton Diptych at the London National Gallery (see Introduction), whose insular origins do not exclude continental—and more specifically Bohemian—influences.

The quadrifoiled border medallions show the bear and the swan which were adopted as emblems by Jean de Berry, as well as the mysterious initials *EV*. With a few slight differences and embellishments, these marks of ownership recur later in the Duke's *Grandes Heures* (Plate 20).

PLATE 14

The Très Belles Heures of Notre Dame
p. 186   *The Way of the Cross*

As previously stated, the 1402 inventory attributed the main responsibility for the decoration of the *Très Belles Heures* to Jacquemart de Hesdin. The mention of his name in the inventory is, in itself, a special tribute to his reputation, for the painter known as the "Brussels Initials Master" (Plate 6) also took an important part in the decoration of this manuscript. Nevertheless, it was Jacquemart who created the paintings that turned this manuscript into a major stepping-stone in the development of the "new style."

The spelling of his birthplace varies from document to document; it is therefore impossible to know exactly whether he was born in Artois, near Calais, or in Hainaut (Belgium), but in any case he was a Northerner. According to the same archival documents, he began working as a painter for Jean de Berry in 1384, at first in Bourges and later in Poitiers. He took part in the decoration of his master's *Petites Heures* (Plate 15) and Psalter (Plate 12). He also worked on a Bible, now in the Vatican Library, which Jean de Berry probably offered to Pope Clement VII. He was also responsible for the large full-page paintings in the *Grandes Heures* (Plate 20) of which, unfortunately, only a single page has survived.

The Way of the Cross which is reproduced here can be taken as a preparation for the one in the *Grandes Heures*. It was visibly inspired by the work of Simone Martini dealing with the same subject, but the influence of other fourteenth-century Italian painters can also be detected in the work of Jacquemart. The fact that the anonymous master who collaborated with him on the decoration of the *Très Belles Heures* and the *Vatican Bible* was doubtless Italian is most enlightening in this respect.

It is altogether possible that he introduced Jacquemart to the artistic formulae that were then in use in his country. Hovever, as Millard Meiss pointed out, Jacquemart deserved credit not only for assimilating, but also in certain instances for "improving," upon the models from which he drew his inspiration. He sacrificed certain effects of rather theatrical pathos in favor of a feeling of space, realism, and measure that were somewhat lacking in Simone Martini's *Way of the Cross*.

PLATE 15

The Petites Heures of Jean De Berry
fol. 97   *The Duke de Berry in Prayer before the Virgin and the Infant Jesus*

Of all the manuscripts Jean de Berry ordered from artists he patronized, the *Petites Heures* probably has the most intriguing history. We cannot even be certain that the manuscript was not begun considerably earlier, for some other great patron, and then later completed for Jean de Berry. The Duke appears on a number of pages, but in extremely different guises, and some of his effigies may have been retouched. Nonetheless, Millard Meiss was of the opinion that the overall decoration of the volume was executed between 1384 and 1390, with the exception of a page painted by the Limbourgs, representing the Duke de Berry leaving his castle on a voyage—that page was probably inserted into the volume around 1412.

Several artists collaborated on the decoration: among them, the "Passion Master" who had, at that point, reached the very end of his career, the great Jacquemart de Hesdin, and a painter who was, for a long time, erroneously confused with him and who later took an active part in the decoration of the *Grandes Heures* (Plate 20). He is known as "Pseudo-Jacquemart."

The part taken in the decoration of these *Petites Heures* by the aging painter and follower of Pucelle, whom Meiss was the first to call the "Passion Master" and whom François Avril justly identified with Jean Le Noir, makes this volume the meeting point par excellence of the old and the new styles of illumination which began competing with each other at the very end of the fourteenth century.

The painting reproduced here is an example of Jacquemart de Hesdin's work at the beginning of his career. His representation of the Virgin with the Infant Jesus appearing to the praying Duke de Berry who is surrounded by his favorite dogs, owes nothing to the Italianizing tradition of Pucelle and his followers. The smiling majesty of the Virgin's delicately molded face relates it, on the contrary, to the new trends from Flanders which were about to completely transform French illumination. We can also detect the influence of contemporary sculpture, whose most famous representative was André Beauneveu.

On the other hand, the beggars painted in the margin of the same page by the "Passion Master" were most directly inspired by the grotesque figures with which Pucelle and his disciples had decorated their most beautiful manuscripts.

BOCCACCIO: CONCERNING FAMOUS WOMEN

Boccaccio's *De mulieribus claris* was translated into French as early as 1401 by an unknown author, who was for a long time erroneously identified as Laurent de Premierfait. The four paintings reproduced here have been selected from the copy Jacques Raponde offered to Philip the Bold, Duke of Burgundy, in 1403–1404. With the exception of pages thirty-three to forty-eight, the illustrations of Philip the Bold's copy were the work of an excellent artist, called the "Coronation Master" by Millard Meiss. The elegant, although slightly mannered style of this painter, his delicate and, at the same time, bright colors, as well as the gracefulness of his subjects with their backgrounds abounding in realistic detail, are typical of the many anonymous illuminators of great talent and outstanding productivity who filled Parisian workshops at the beginning of the fifteenth century.

A. fol. 39   *"The Story of Procris, Cephalus' Beautiful Wife."*

A rival had hinted to Cephalus that his wife preferred riches to his person. He therefore arranged for a confidant to tempt her, and she agreed to come to a rendezvous in exchange for costly presents. Overcome with remorse she then fled into the forest, where Cephalus, who was out hunting, inadvertently killed her with an arrow. The painting unites in a single image the temptation of Procris and the tragic hunt.

B. fol. 69   *"The Story of Pamphile, Daughter of Plateus."*

According to the legend retold by Boccaccio, this ingenious woman first had the idea of collecting "on the branches of bushes the small fleeces of the worms that make silk," and after cleansing, winding, and spinning them, she made fabrics out of these cocoons. The illustration shows curious little creatures with feet; the painter obviously having confused the silk worms with their product. It should be noted how precisely the loom has been depicted here, as well as in the following reproduction.

C. fol. 86   *"Thamyris, the Most Noble Artist."*

The illustrator had little trouble finding a model for this scene since, at that time, many women worked as illuminators. Here, the *peintresse* is seated before her easel, working on a panel of the Virgin and the Divine Child. Behind her, an assistant with a pestle is grinding colors in a mortar. In the foreground, on a table, is a small assortment of brushes and jars.

D. fol. 71   *"The Story of Gaia, Wife of King Tarquinus."*

This Roman Queen was a model of the finest domestic virtues and didn't consider it beneath her to spin and weave wool with her ladies. We see her here with a crown on her head, but an apron around her waist, sitting at her loom. Close to her, the wool is being combed by one woman, carded by another, and spun by a third.

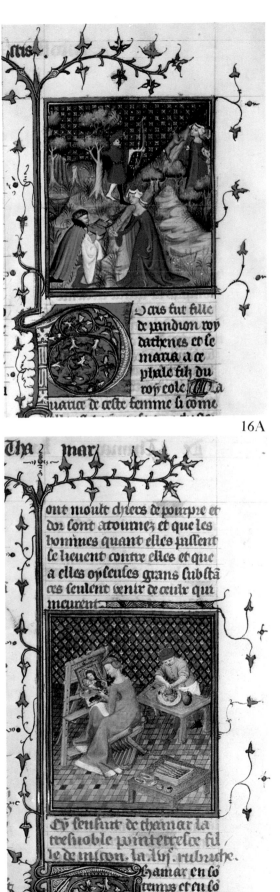

aris fut fille
de pandion roy
dathenes et se
maria a ce
phale filz du
roy cole Ma
quance de ceste femme li co...

16A

Cy apres sensuit lystoire
de pamphile fille de platee.
La .xliiiᵉ. rubriche.

Amphile femme
moult noble se
lon les ancien
nes hystoires
fut du pays de
grece et ne trou
uons pas de quelle cite ne de quel
territoire. Mais nous a...

16B

ont moult chiers de pourpre et
dor sont atournez et que les
hommes quant elles passent
se lieuent contre elles et que
a elles oyseuses grans substa
ces seulent venir de ceulx qui
meurent.

Cy sensuit de thamar la
tresnoble paintetresse fil
le de micon. la .lvj. rubriche.

hamar en so
temps et en so
aage fut tres
noble paintre
resse et se il est
ainsi que le
grant temps nous ait oste

16C

e gaye a tille
iassoit ce que
ne nay pas co
gnoissance
par aucunes
hystoires de
quelle paiente elle fut ne de
quel lignie. Toutenoies te...

16D

Le vous du miracle qui auint a seue la
messe en lombardie en leue de son trespasse
ment par les merites mouss saint denis de
france

n celui temps flourissoit
a paris philosophie a tou
te clergie y estoit bi estu
des des bij ars si hante
z en si grant auctorite q
len ne treuue pas que il fust onques si plenteis
ne si ferueus en athenes ne en egipte ne a rome
ne en nulles des pties du monde si nestoit
pas tant seulement pour la delitablete du
lieu ne pour la plante des biens qui en la cite
habondent aiais pour la puis a pour la fran
chise que le bon roy lors auoit touslours por
tee a que le roy phe son fils portoit aus mais
a aus escoliers a toute luniuersite. Sy ne li
soit on pas tant seulement en celle noble cite
des bij sciences liberaux aiais de decres a de
lois a de phisique a sur toutes les autres estoit
leue par plus grant ferueur a par plus
grant estude la sainte paige de theologie.
En ce temps estudioit a paris vne dei
nez de leuesche de chartres dune ville qui
a nom boues si auoit nom amaurys il
estoit grans clers a souttieus en lart de loi
que quant il ot longuement leu en icel art

il fu martirez saint lutier euesque dosauns
Le vous coment ebroins fut ocis
z coment pepins ly brisez qui fu pere
charles martel fut maistre du palais
En ce vols comencent les fais du
noble roy charles martel a coment
il eschapa de la prison sa marrastre
a coment il fut prince de deuls royaume
Le vols coment charles martel
occist en vne bataille iiij lxxxxv sar
rasins a coment il tolly les dismes
aus eglises
Le xxvij coment charle martel re
couura la cite dauignon a les autres
cites que sarrazins auoient prinses a
coment il morut
En ce xxviij comencent les fais le
roy pepin a coment grisfons le tiers filz
charles martel guerroia ses freres a
coment charlemaine deuint moines a
coment ly rois pepins fut couronnez
Le vois coment li rois pepins con
tint des lombars qui tenoient le
rsse de rome a de la guerre le duc
trusfier
Le xxx coment le duc trusfier
fut ocis a de la mort le roy pepin

Coment la monarchie des iiij roy
aumes vint toute en la main le roy
cloths a come il assolt les lombars
du tien qui deuoiet a de ses meurs

PLATE 17

The Grandes Chroniques De France

The main interest of this volume is not its text—of which there are many copies in existence — but the conditions of its material execution. We know from the 1402 inventory of Jean de Berry's books (Plates 26 and 27) that it belonged to the Duke's collection at that time, and that it had probably been acquired shortly before that date from the executors of the estate of Aimeri de Rochechouart, who died in 1397 and whose arms it bears.

The marginal decoration, consisting of branches with tri-lobed leaves which also appear in the letters, is decidedly French; one might even say Parisian if this type of decoration had not been so widespread at the time. However, the illustration of the text is definitely not the work of a French artist. Although these small scenes are, by their overall composition, very similar to those produced in great numbers by Parisian workshops at the very beginning of the fifteenth century (they may be compared especially to the Boccaccio illustrations on Plate 16), the rather crude faces, as well as the boldly contrasting colors of the attire, betray a foreign artist, probably Bohemian. The small florets which burst from each corner of the paintings and the small dots in groups of three which accompany them are also of foreign inspiration. Thus, we may consider this volume a relatively modest, but all the more interesting, example of the fusion of different contributions which compose the "International Style" as it was found in Parisian manuscripts at the turn of the fourteenth into the fifteenth century.

A. fol. 77   *King Clotharius II Receiving the Ambassadors of the King of the Lombards.*

This depiction of the Merovingian sovereign might be compared to that of the Emperor Charlemagne in the German manuscript of the *Sachsenspiegel*, a page of which is reproduced on Plate 35.

B. fol. 295   *A Class at the University of Paris.*

This image of a professor seated at his lectern, dispensing his knowledge to an audience of respectable age (whose academic hoods could indicate that they are all graduates) symbolizes the prestige which, according to the *Grandes Chroniques*, was enjoyed by the University of Paris during the reign of Philippe Auguste. The beginning of the chapter which this painting illustrates stresses without modesty that "philosophy and all the sciences flourished in Paris" at that time, and that the study of the seven liberal arts was more advanced there than it had ever been "in Athens, Egypt, Rome, or any other place in the world."

PLATE 18

The Works of Christine De Pisan
fol. 35

Christine de Pisan was born in 1384, the daughter of an astrologer at the court of Charles V. Married at the age of fifteen and widowed eleven years later, she found herself with three children to support. Responding to the change in her circumstances, and aided by her innate genius, she became the first Frenchwoman to live by her pen and to organize the diffusion of her writings with method and competence. Shortly after 1405 all of her existing works were collected in the present manuscript, which was probably intended for Louis of Orléans; after his murder it was acquired by Jean de Berry.

The best part of the illustration is the work of an extremely original artist whose activity in Paris seems to have been limited to about ten years—and exclusively to the writings of Christine de Pisan. For the illustration of this manuscript, a page of which has been reproduced here, he sought the assistance of a much more prolific painter generally known as the "Egerton Master" (Plate 6). Since the most interesting series of illustrations inserted into Christine's texts is the one dealing with the *Epître d'Othéa*, the illuminator of this series has been called the "Epître Master."

His compositions differ so widely in style and technique from the Parisian productions of his time that one has often been tempted to assume that he was of foreign origin. Although we cannot be certain that Jean Porcher is right when he suggests that the "Epître Master" came from Lombardy, it is nonetheless probable that he was familiar with Lombard illumination. His light, transparent colors, his extensive use of white, the proportions of his large figures, his taste for geometric composition and for motifs borrowed from Antiquity hitherto unknown in France, all give his paintings an Italian, or Italianate, mood, in which influences from Tuscany and Padua can also be detected.

A. *The Wheel of Fortune.*

The teaching which the Goddess Othéa reveals to Hector in her *Epître* is presented as a series of moral precepts which are developed in the subsequent "commentary" and illustrated with examples from history; they give the full measure of Christine de Pisan's great erudition and are, moreover, imbued with a Christian meaning by what the author calls an "allegory." The subject of the Wheel of Fortune, that perverse goddess who raises man to the highest honors only to precipitate him to the depths a moment later, has been abundantly treated by medieval iconography.

B. *The Treachery of Worldly Delights.*

The text reminds us that happiness, such as the "Epicureans" conceived it, is actually not worthy of the name, because it is a fleeting illusion. In keeping with a well-established tradition, the vain search for "worldly" happiness is, in this instance, depicted by the seductions of a love which, although extremely chaste in its representation, is nonetheless of an essentially carnal nature.

sus autrui premierement. Car nous ne
sauons de quel courage sont les choses fai-
tes lesquelles condampnez cest grant pre-
sompcion Et le deuons interpreter en la meil
leur partie. Secondement car nous ne
sommes pas certains quelz seront ceulx q
a present sont bons ou mauuais. A ce pro-
pos dist nostre seigneur en leuangille. Noli
te iudicare et non iudicabimini. Inquo ei
iudicio iudicaueritis iudicabimini. ma-
thei septimo capitulo.

Fortune selon la maniere de parler des poe-
etes puet bien estre appellee la grant deesse. Car par elle nous veons le cours des choses mondaines tourner et pour ce q elle pro-
met a maint assez prosperitez et de fait en
donne a autrui et les retoult en petit de
heure quant il lui plaist dit au bon cheualier
q il ne se doit fier en ses promesses ne de son
fortier en ses aduersitez. et dit saintes les
tours de fortune sont quasi enuimes

Car ce q il dit que il ne se doit fier en fortune pouons entendre q le bon esperit doit fu-
ir et despriser les delices du monde de ce dit bo-
ece ou tiers liure de consolacion q la felicite des
epicuriens doit estre appellee infelicite car cest
la vraye plaine et parfaite felicite qui puet lome
faire souffisant puissant reuerend solempnel
et ioyeulx lesquelz choses ne presient point
les choses ou les mondains mettet leur felicite
par ce dit dieu p le prophete populus meus qui te
beatu dicut ipi te decipiunt. ysaie iij. c.

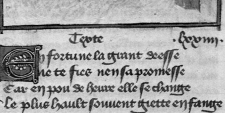

En fortune la grant deesse
Ne te fies nen sa promesse
Car en pou de heure elle se change
Le plus hault souuent iette en fange

parmeno seruus. philocis meretrix. Syra anus.

lach   me
Euer si queret me. modo isle dicatos ad
                    ad inuestigandum
par.   portum percontatum aduentum pam

phili audin quid dicam syra. si que

lach   isle   me
rit me. ut rium dicas. si non querit nullus dixeris
alia die   ut   sce
alias ut uti possim caulabie integra, sed undeon

PLATE 19

The Comedies of Terence
fol. 210   *A Scene from "Hecyra" (The Mother-in-Law): Parmeno, a Slave; Philotis, a Courtesan; Syra, an Old Woman*

A certain number of classical Latin texts were copied and richly decorated in Paris at the beginning of the fifteenth century. Of these, three remarkable copies of Terence's *Comedies* have survived to this day.

The most famous of these three manuscripts is known as the *Terence of the Dukes*, in memory of two of its successive owners. It is not certain whether the volume was initially intended for Crown Prince Louis, Duke of Guyenne, but he owned it when he died in 1415. At that time, his confessor, Jean d'Arsonval, gave the book to Jean de France, Duke de Berry, who was the deceased's great-uncle.

For several centuries no manuscripts containing Terence's works had been illustrated. Consequently, the illuminators commissioned to decorate new copies of the *Comedies* had to show a truly creative spirit in order to accomplish their difficult task. It is not impossible that one or the other of them may have had access to copies of Terence that had been illustrated during the Carolingian period, imitating Antique manuscripts that have since been lost; but if this were the case, they did not allow themselves to be influenced by such archaic models. On the other hand, it seems certain that the erudite director of a workshop closely guided the artists who illuminated, before 1408, a copy of Terence that was presented to the Duke de Berry (Bibl. Nat. Ms. Lat., 7907A), since marginal annotations, which can be deciphered with ultraviolet rays, give precise descriptions of the personages to be depicted, down to their social condition and their costume. It was probably this manuscript that served, somewhat later, as a model for the painters who illustrated the *Terence of the Dukes*.

The most important of the collaborating artists is called the "Luçon Master," because of a Missal he decorated for Etienne Loypeau, Bishop of Luçon. Among other paintings, he must be credited with the frontispiece of the *Terence of the Dukes*, an imitation of the frontispiece in Ms. Lat. 7907A by the first Josephus Master (Plate 21).

However, the present reproduction of the scene from *Hecyra* is the work of the master who collaborated in the decoration of a beautiful manuscript of the *Histoires d'Orose* (Bibl. Nat. Ms. Fr. 301). The central motif of the painting is formed by the beautiful courtesan Philotis, standing between the figures of the slave Parmeno and old Syra. Her fringed dress and extravagant headgear leave no doubt as to her profession.

THE GRANDES HEURES OF JEAN DE BERRY
fol. 96   *Saint Peter Receives Jean de Berry in Paradise*

In 1409, after many long months of work, the Duke de Berry's "workers" completed a Book of Hours more splendid than any of the volumes which that indefatigable book lover had added previously to his collection.

Several artists of widely different temperaments were entrusted with the decoration of this book. Some of them did not work exclusively for the Duke, but were also active in the Parisian workshops that produced so many remarkable volumes during the first years of the fifteenth century.

It is rather puzzling to note that quite a few of the medium-size paintings which mark the beginning of each office are faithful copies (although on a different scale) of models found in older volumes belonging to the Duke. The same holds true for many of the grotesque marginal figures which imitate original creations drawn by Jean Pucelle for the *Belleville Breviary* and the *Hours of Jeanne d'Évreux*. In the same "retrospective" spirit, the first Calendar of the *Grandes Heures* reproduces the iconographic theme created by Pucelle which had previously been repeated in the *Petites Heures* of Jean de Berry (Plate 15).

Seventeen full-page paintings, most likely the work of Jacquemart de Hesdin, contributed to the exceptional character of the volume. Unfortunately they were cut out, at some unspecified time, and have all disappeared, with the exception of a single leaf (whose origin was only recently determined), now kept in the Louvre Museum.

The painting which decorates the left column of the page reproduced here shows Saint Peter welcoming Jean de Berry at the door of a chapel symbolizing the gates of Paradise. The Duke is accompanied by several kinsmen—among them we recognize almost with certainty: Philip the Bold, Duke of Burgundy (deceased 1404), Louis II, Duke of Anjou, and possibly the Duke of Bavaria, father of Queen Isabeau, wife of Charles VI of France. The anonymous artist, who was also responsible for many of the paintings associated with the so-called Bedford group tactfully portrayed Jean de Berry as an old grey-haired man, to stress the fact that he was portraying a scene in the distant future. In the decorated initial directly below, the Duke is depicted as considerably younger: he seems to be having a vision of the happy fate awaiting him in the world beyond.

The poly-lobed medallions in the margins abound with leaves, flowers, butterflies, and birds; they are decorated with Jean de Berry's arms ("of France, the edges engrailed with gules"), his emblems (the bear and the wounded swan, chosen as a play on words—*ours*, "bear" plus *cygne*, "swan," equals the name of the mysterious *Ursine* of whom the Duke was said to have been enamored), and the initials *E V* of uncertain meaning *(En Vous?)*. His motto, "The time will come," is inscribed on banners which twine around the plant shoots that link the medallions.

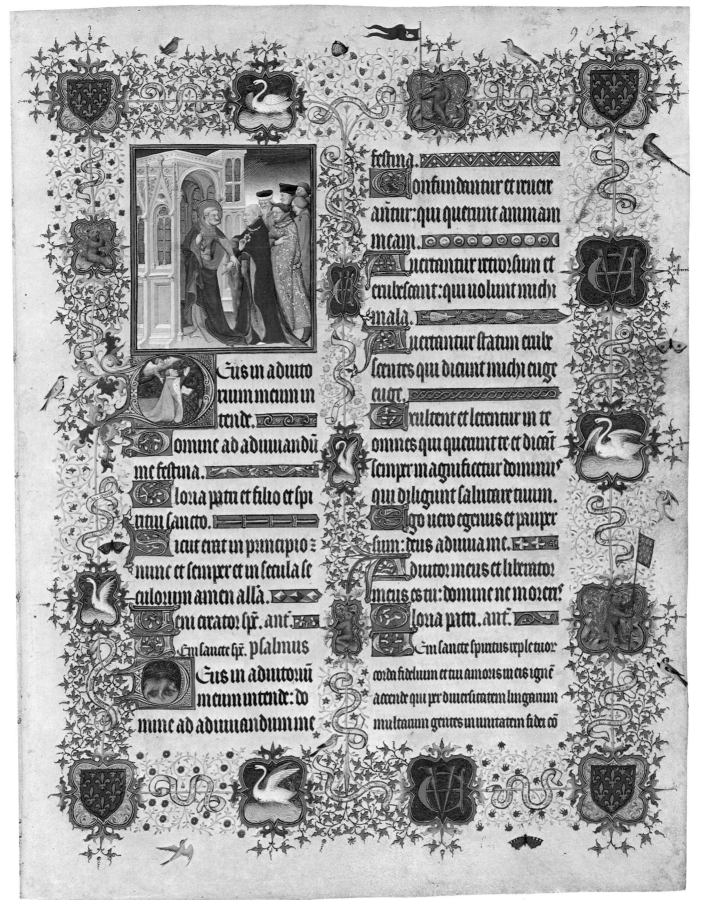

PLATE 21

JOSEPHUS: THE HISTORY OF THE JEWS
fol. 25   *The Story of Joseph*

The Jewish historian Flavius Josephus (approximately A.D. 37 to 100) composed an important work about the history of his people, based mainly upon the Old Testament. Under Charles V, the Latin original was translated into French and rather widely read. Jean de Berry had two copies in his library. One of them, a page of which is reproduced here, was copied for him around 1415, but his death interrupted the completion of the illustration. It was finished at a much later date by the great Fouquet.

Of the three paintings existing in the manuscript at the time of Jean de Berry's death, two were the work of a remarkable artist; a note in the manuscript, written about the middle of the fifteenth century, calls him "the Duke de Berry's illuminator." However, his imprint cannot be found in any other volume executed for the Duke. The frontispiece of the *Terence*, offered to the Duke de Berry by his treasurer Martin Gouge, Bishop of Chartres, (Paris, Bibl. Nat., Ms. Lat. 7907A) is decidedly by the same artist, but that volume was a workshop production which only happened to become a part of the Duke's collection. No other work by this rather unprolific artist has come down to us—at best a few pages of a Book of Hours in the British Library may be associated with his style.

The pastel tones, favored by this newcomer to the circle of Parisian illuminators, link him to Jacquemart de Hesdin, but he designed his figures according to the Italian principles elaborated during the preceding century, while trying to create a visual revival in his compositions of Antiquity and the Orient. His concern with local color, even though whimsical, is obvious—although such a preoccupation was rare in his time.

Here we see the first episodes of the story of Joseph, closely following the text in Genesis 38. Joseph is sent to his brothers, who are grazing their cattle in the plains of Dothan. Later, they throw him into an empty cistern, and finally sell him as a slave to traders who take him to Egypt, on the other side of the Red Sea.

The painter's taste for the exotic expresses itself in the costumes and faces of the traders into whose hands Joseph has been delivered. We may even speculate as to whether the artist may have used models from the Near East for his figures, some of which clearly recall Persian paintings. At any rate, the camels of the caravaneers have been depicted with the highest accuracy—he didn't have to look far for a live model, since the Duke de Berry kept a camel in his menagerie. In the deep blue sky which contrasts sharply with the scarlet waters of the Red Sea, he inserted a flight of storks, as though to prove that he knew perfectly well that these migratory birds spend the winter on the other side of the Mediterranean.

ti ence le secod liure des anachetes
des uits selo la sentece de ioseph.
Dzes la mozt de ysaac
ses filz deuiserent entre
ulx les tabernacles. non
pas ceulx quilz auoient
pzins et tenus. Mais esau donna
a son frere la cite de hebzon. il habito

ut en seir. et regnoit en ydumee. La
quelle il appella ainsi par son nom.
Il la nomma edom la quelle nun
pzon elle a eu pour cause quil y cha
oit. Auanes fois quant il esto
ut enfant et il auoit fam il retour
noit par la et son frere li appareillo
ut le potage. cestoit pzee pour disner

PLATE 22

GASTON PHÉBUS, COUNT OF FOIX: THE BOOK OF HUNTING
fol. 67   *The Gathering before the Stag Hunt*

Gaston III, Count of Foix and Béarn (1331–1391), owes his lasting posthumous renown far more to the substantial hunting treatise he composed from May 1387 to the end of 1388, than to his vain attempts at establishing his hegemony over the entire Pyrénées region. He was a passionate hunter of great experience, familiar with every kind of game, at home as well as in Sweden, Norway, and East Prussia, where he traveled extensively. He had, moreover, read every book on hunting available at the time, and the one he composed toward the end of his life proves that his talents as a naturalist were equal to his gifts as a hunter.

His treatise became extremely popular, and a number of copies have survived to this day, translated into various languages. The page reproduced here belongs to a copy that surely must be considered the most beautiful of all. It probably was executed around 1407, and perhaps intended for Jean sans Peur, Duke of Burgundy; it was illustrated in one of the Parisian workshops which Millard Meiss grouped together under the designation of the "Bedford trend," since its style heralds the "Bedford Master."

The artists of this group—and in particular the illustrator of the *Adelphi* in the *Terence of the Dukes* (Plate 19)—all painted the same truculent figures, full of life and movement. Their stocky silhouettes and bulb-nosed faces recall the art of the Netherlands, but the molded flow of their dress links them (still according to Millard Meiss) to the Italo-Avignon tradition of Simone Martini.

One of the painters who collaborated on the decoration of *The Book of Hunting* shows here the gathering of all participants for a meal which preceded the "slipping of the hounds" onto a stag. During a joyful picnic, the huntsmen come to report to their master, surrounded by his guests. Since dawn, the "beaters" have been scouting various sectors of the forest to locate animals worthy of being "brought to bay." They show him the traces which they have picked up and tell him about the tracks they have followed, by which they have deduced the age of the animals. The master then decides which animal is to be pursued.

In an enclosure on the left, the horses patiently wait for their riders. The hounds are gathered near a spring, where servants have placed gourds and jugs to cool. They will be unleashed shortly when the signal is given to "slip the hounds."

Cy deuise comment lassemblee se doit faire en este et en yuer.

a quele al   separer lun de lautre. et lun ne
semblee se   doit point venir sus la queste
fait en tele   de lautre ne faire enuay. Et
maniere   chascun doit quester en la ma
la nuyt de   niere que iay dit du uncle quil
uant que le   puet. et leur doit assigner le
seigneur   lieu ou lassemblee sera au plus
de la chace ou le maistre veneur   aysie de tous et au plus pres
uouldra aler en boys. Il doit fai   de leurs questes. Et doit estre
re venir deuant luy les veneurs   le lieu ou lassemblee sera en
les aydes les varles et les pages.   vn biau pre bien vert ou il ait
et leur doit a chascun assigner   biaulx arbres tout au tour.
leurs questes en certain lieu. et   lun loing de lautre. et vne fo

PLATE 23

THE BEDFORD HOURS
fol. 257   *The Duchess of Bedford and her Patron Saint Anne*

John of Lancaster, the third son of King Henry IV of England, was born in 1389 and became Duke of Bedford in 1414. At the death of his brother, Henry V, he became Regent of the Kingdoms of England and France. (England did not recognize the sovereignty of Charles VII over France.) He died in Rouen in 1435, in the very place where he had had Joan of Arc condemned and executed only shortly before.

He had a pronounced taste for French manuscripts, perhaps stimulated by his marriage in 1423 to Anne of Burgundy, the third daughter of Jean sans Peur. During his visits to France he patronized one of the most prolific Parisian workshops, today known as the "Bedford workshop" in memory of its illustrious client.

The Duke most probably ordered a Book of Hours for Parisian use on the occasion of his marriage; the page reproduced here is well known. The arms, mottoes, and portraits of the couple recur in a number of places.

On this page, the main painting shows the Duchess kneeling before her Patron Saint, Anne, at whose side can be seen the Virgin with the Infant Jesus. The old man leaning against an empty chair in the right of the painting is probably Saint Joseph. On the drapery, upheld by angels, which forms the background of the scene can be read the motto [*Je*] *suis contente* ("[I] am content").

The lateral and lower margins of the page follow a decorative principle that was made fashionable by the "Boucicaut Master" and his workshop: several medallions, each dedicated to a particular theme. As indicated on the small scrolls, they represent from top to bottom and from left to right the three successive husbands of Saint Anne: Joachim, Cleophas, and Salome, as well as Saint Anne's other two daughters (besides the Virgin) both also named Mary, who are shown conversing with their husbands, Alphaeus and Zebediah.

These subjects, which stress the notion of marriage, are particularly appropriate, and add weight to the theory that the volume was executed at the time of the Bedford marriage around 1423.

PLATE 24

THE BELLES HEURES OF JEAN DE BERRY
fol. 97   *Saint Bruno and his Companions Enter the Grande Chartreuse*

Some time after 1404, three brothers named Paul, Jean, and Herman de Limbourg ceased working as painters for the Duke of Burgundy and entered the exclusive service of Jean de Berry. Their family name, of Dutch origin, was to become known as that of the most talented painters of their generation. Around 1408–1409 they completed the decoration of a magnificent volume which was listed as the *Belles Heures* in the inventory of the Duke's library and, after his death, it passed into the hands of Yolande of Aragon. The remarkable series of paintings with which they embellished the volume already expresses their originality and the mastery of their extremely personal art, which found its culmination in the *Très Riches Heures* (Plates 26 and 27).

The iconographic subjects they chose—or were asked—to develop for the *Belles Heures* were quite uncommon; some of them have actually no known precedent. The paintings dedicated to these subjects have been grouped in a certain number of independent cycles and, instead of the habitual liturgical texts they are accompanied by excerpts—most taken from the *Golden Legend*.

The page reproduced here belongs to the third of these cycles which tells the story of Diocrès, an eleventh-century theologian who became the teacher of Saint Bruno, founder of the Carthusian order.

The painter, whom Millard Meiss identified as Paul, the oldest of the three brothers, depicted Saint Bruno and his companions entering the first Carthusian monastery which they have just finished building. On the left, a layman is about to follow them: he has been tonsured, but is still wearing a blue smock and boots, instead of the monastic habit. One of the Saint's companions is shown in the process of pulling the robe over his head, which is hidden. This pleasantly realistic detail is typical of the Limbourgs' taste for the picturesque, and also of their prodigious craftsmanship.

The "austere mountains," upon which the monastery was built, are represented by a jagged peak; it stands out, a massive green shape, against a checkered background of blue and gold. The back of the same page shows an idealized representation of the monastery.

The artist's perfect mastery gives his composition the rhythm of a slow procession; its sculptural character has been enhanced by the uniformly white tonality of the monks' robes. One can feel that the artist took pleasure in showing off his virtuosity by almost totally depriving himself of the glamour of color: it is the subtle modulation of the white robes that makes this scene so effective.

Et eos non sine grandi labore ad locum ubi. vij.
stelle q̄s uidēt in sopnio steterāt duxit et ait. hic
erit locus uester: ibi igitur ipō epō uiuo scō uiuā
te edificare cepūt p̄mā domū ordis cartusiensiū.

PLATE 25

THE BELLES HEURES OF JEAN DE BERRY
fol. 191   *A Young Christian Heroically Resists Temptation, In the Presence of Saint
Paul the Hermit*

This painting is the first of eight the Limbourgs dedicated to the life of the Hermit-Saints, Paul and Anthony, as related in the *Golden Legend*. We are told that, at the time of the persecution under the Emperor Decius, a young Christian was taken to a "place of pleasure" and exposed to the shameless caresses of a woman, which his chains kept him from warding off. In order to resist the carnal pleasure that was rising within him despite himself, he bit off his tongue. Saint Paul witnessed the incident, which so horrified him that he fled into the desert.

The *Golden Legend* describes in greater detail than shown by the painter the "place of pleasure" where this edifying, although lascivious scene took place. The artist left out the birds and flowers mentioned in the text, and he has the young Christian lying on the ground rather than on "a soft bed." However, "the murmur of water" is indicated by the stone fountain which forms the central piece in the painting.

The woman who is "as impure as she is beautiful" and is supposed to "sully the flesh" of the young man as ordered by the Emperor, works at her shameless mission without a smile—the picture of professional indifference. Her provocatively elegant dress and supple grace recall the charming little creatures with whom certain painters had illustrated the two manuscripts of Boccaccio's *Concerning Famous Women* a few years earlier (Plate 16).

The young man's hands have been tied behind his back; he has heroically bitten off his tongue and—in a spurt of bright red blood—is spitting it into the face of his all-too seductive tormentor. The contraction of his features has been perfectly rendered, and fully expresses the superhuman effort he has had to make to resist the temptress.

On the right, Saint Paul—already depicted with a halo and hermit's robe, although he had not yet fled from Rome—reacts to this horrifying scene with a gesture of outrage. The man whose torso appears on the extreme right might be Saint Anthony, Saint Paul's future desert companion, but the Emperor Decius would be a more plausible candidate, since he seems to be clad in armor.

The trees in the foreground of the painting and next to the fountain have been systematically reduced in size, so as not to conceal the figures. This device, which adds depth to the composition and prefigures the "birds-eye-view" principle, had already been used during the preceding century, mainly by the *Maître aux Boqueteaux*.

Sanct? paul? primi hemita feruete psecucoe de
ay uiso q? xpianus quida me amena ligat et
ab ipudica ffitat? lingua abscidit et mea faciem
spuit ut temptacone dolo? fugaret. roma fug?

PLATE 26

THE TRÈS RICHES HEURES OF JEAN DE BERRY
fol. 4   *Calendar: The Month of April*

The volume listed as the *Très Riches Heures* in the inventory of Jean de Berry's possessions compiled following his death is today the pride of the Condé Museum in Chantilly. It certainly is one of the most famous manuscripts in the world. This masterpiece of illumination, which the Limbourg brothers were unable to finish since they died shortly after their protector in 1416, does have a composite aspect because other artists, especially the famous Jean Colombe, continued working on the decoration until the end of the fifteenth century, under extremely obscure conditions. Nonetheless, it is to the genius of the Limbourgs that the manuscript owes its universal fame and exceptional artistic interest.

Its iconographic and stylistic relation to the *Belles Heures* (Plates 24 and 25) is obvious, but so is the artistic progress the three artists had made in only a few years span. Further detailed studies of Italian and Antique art had allowed them to emancipate themselves more and more from the traditional models of religious imagery and to create a new, extremely personal style. As Millard Meiss so aptly put it, "like the Boucicaut Master they were able to fuse the apparently irreconcilable values of Italy and the Netherlands into a harmonious, original synthesis."

In keeping with tradition, the series of the offices in the *Très Riches Heures* is preceded by a Calendar; its illustrations depict the twelve months of the year. In this instance, however, the Calendar resolutely differs from customary precedents. Each month furnishes a subject for a full-page painting, inspired by everyday life, with more or less direct allusions to Jean de Berry, his kin, and his castles. Above the paintings, the zodiacal signs are inscribed in a semicircle, accompanied by exceptionally precise astronomical information.

Here, the month of April is symbolized by a betrothal scene. The figures clearly belong to the princely class, or at least to the aristocracy, and it may well be that the painter wanted to portray the engagement of Charles d'Orléans to Bonne d'Armagnac, Jean de Berry's granddaughter. At any rate, in the background, the castle of Dourdan, which had been owned by Jean de Berry since 1400, is clearly recognizable.

The elegant mannerism of this courtly art recalls the Italian style, as well as a number of techniques favored by the Paris workshops around 1400–1405. This allows us — according to Millard Meiss — to attribute this particular painting to Jean de Limbourg, rather than to his brothers Paul or Herman.

PLATE 27

THE TRÈS RICHES HEURES OF JEAN DE BERRY
fol. 25   *The Temptation and the Fall*

This illustration of an episode from Genesis dealing with the sin of our first ancestors and their expulsion from Paradise is completely unusual in a Book of Hours. It was painted on the back of a blank page and placed opposite the *Annunciation* which, on the following page, begins the Hours of the Virgin. Throughout the Middle Ages, theology and iconography often developed and illustrated such concepts linking original sin to the conception of the Savior, the "new Adam," whose sacrifice on the Cross redeemed our first father's fault.

Paradise on earth is represented here as an orchard: fruit trees setting off a lush meadow filled with flowers. In the center rises a fountain with delicate arcades that ease its imposing dimensions; it recalls the "wells of life" we often find in manuscripts produced between the eighth and eleventh centuries. A golden wall encloses the Garden of Eden, itself surrounded by barren mountain slopes. The mysterious blue waves rising either from an ocean or from a sea of clouds contribute to the dreamlike mood of the painting, a perfect rendering of its subject.

Four successive episodes of the biblical narration have been grouped here into a single space. From left to right, we see Eve tempted by the demon, who has borrowed some of the first woman's most gracious attributes, the better to seduce her. Next, Eve offers the forbidden fruit to Adam; the painting ingeniously shows him "being led astray" from his duty by the sexual charms of his mate. Further on, God the Father accuses the culprits of their sin and announces their punishment.

On the extreme right an angel, the color of flames, metes out the punishment: he forces our first ancestors to depart through the gates of Paradise and to climb down the mountains they'll never be able to climb back up again; they try to hide their nudity — of which they have now become ashamed.

Even more successfully than in *The Martyrdom of Saint Catherine* in the *Belles Heures*, the Limbourgs have endowed Eve's feminine nudity with a discreet but powerful eroticism which is enhanced by the perfection of the exquisite design. The pose of Adam accepting the apple is truly a graphic "tour de force" and it is most likely intentional that his genitals are not concealed. The artist's inspiration was probably derived from a model of Antiquity, or perhaps the synthesis of several such models.

PLATE 28

THE BOUCICAUT HOURS
fol. 142   *Funeral Service*

The beginning of the fifteenth century was marked by the appearance in Paris of an artist of exceptional talent. Together with the Limbourg brothers, he ranks among the very best of those who imparted a hitherto unknown vigor to the art of illumination.

Durrieu at first tended to identify him with Jacques Coene, a painter from Bruges who, in 1398, passed his formulas for color preparation on to an Italian named Alcherius before he began working on the plans for the Milan cathedral in 1399. In 1404 he illuminated a Bible for Philip the Bold which, unfortunately, has been lost. Several of the arguments upon which Durrieu based his theory are no longer acceptable today; still, this is a most plausible notion, and has been given renewed impact recently by a number of disconcerting coincidences noted by Millard Meiss.

The first masterpiece by the painter who is most often referred to as the "Boucicaut Master," was the superb volume which he and a number of collaborators executed for Jean le Meingre, Marshall of Boucicaut, between 1401 and 1408.

For a period of time, the Marshall of Boucicaut held the office of Governor of Genoa, having arrived there in 1401; it is therefore altogether plausible that he may have met this decidedly Northern artist in Italy and ordered this Book of Hours from him. It is, moreover, extremely interesting to note that this artist decorated another Book of Hours for a Visconti, and that a merchant from Lucca later bought a Missal from him. These two incidents alone would suffice as proof of the "Boucicaut Master's" contacts with Italy, further confirmed by the Italian influences readily apparent in his artistic concepts.

The "Boucicaut Master" was responsible for many highly important innovations in French illumination. Panofsky has called him "the pioneer of naturalism," since he knew far better than his predecessors how to use the laws of perspective to create three-dimensional impressions on a flat surface. A luminous golden mist blurs the distances in his landscapes which show the transformations that forms undergo when viewed at a distance. Here, a skillfully composed funeral service takes place under the arches of a religious edifice, whose complexity betrays the artist's fascination with architectural problems. His use of muted colors intentionally creates an atmosphere of sadness; the red of the arches boldly contrasts with the black of the garments and the grey and violet of the walls.

PLATE 29

PIERRE SALMON: REPLIES TO CHARLES VI AND COMPLAINS TO THE KING ABOUT HIS CONDITION

fol. 53   *The Author Visits the Royal Palace to Dedicate his Book to his Sovereign*

The "Boucicaut Master" headed an extremely active workshop. It is not easy to distinguish his own (relatively rare) works from the abundant production of his collaborators, who had developed an extremely homogeneous style. The "Boucicaut Master" seems to have played only a minor part in the decoration of this manuscript; even though it must have been a dedication copy, he seems to have only guided the work of his collaborators.

The text of the volume is a political treatise, composed in 1409 by Pierre Salmon (nicknamed *Le Fruitier*) at the request of King Charles VI. Since another version was written shortly afterward (Plate 30), we may assume that the present copy—a page of which is reproduced here—dates from around 1410. Many of the illustrations are the work of the "*Cité des Dames* Master" whose style differs greatly from the Boucicaut workshop, and displays, moreover, a surprising precocity. It makes one wonder whether the manuscript had perhaps not originally remained uncompleted and then been finished a few years later by a different workshop. However, this hypothesis would eliminate the notion that it had, indeed, been presented to the King.

The present painting shows the King accepting from the author the work he has ordered; like many nonreligious scenes painted in the workshop of the "Boucicaut Master," it reflects a definite anecdotal taste. Without any particular coherence, a number of small scenes have been grouped and distributed throughout the various sections of a somewhat strange edifice that is supposed to be the royal palace. A stairway links the upper floor to a paved inner courtyard surrounded by walls topped with turrets. The upper floor is open like a loggia, to show the figures grouped in the throne room: the King, the author, and the Duke de Berry, recognizable by his ample swan-embroidered robe (Plate 26). He is admiring a jewel on the throat of a man with whom he is engaged in conversation.

In the courtyard, an usher armed with his mace guards the entrance to the stairway; an armed rider holds the reins of a mule which Pierre Salmon probably used for his transportation; a servant carries a platter; two unknown persons chat. At the back gate two visitors request entrance from the doorkeeper; two onlookers idly gape; a steward goes to fetch water, or wine. In the garret windows, the heads of small figures seem to be enjoying the fresh air. Flowerpots placed on a windowsill give the painting a picturesque touch of realism.

With total disregard for the laws of perspective, the size of the various personages increases with the distance that separates them from the foreground, and also with their rank and the importance of the role they play in the scene.

y senfuuient les lamentacions Salmon pour au
cunes mezueilles a lui auenues ou pelermage
de ce monde z les epistres pour ce par lui baillees
et enuoiees a tresexcellent z trespuissant prince

PLATE 30

Pierre Salmon: Questions Asked By King Charles VI [. . . and Salmon's Replies]
fol. 4   *Kings Charles VI Conversing with the Author*

In 1412 at the earliest, Pierre Salmon completed another version of his work (Plate 29). For diplomatic reasons the author muted his sympathies for the House of Burgundy, expressed in the initial version, and he also made a few additions.

The manuscript of his new text is kept in the Public and University Library in Geneva, and is more than probably a dedication copy. In any case, it was excuted for King Charles VI, since the King's emblems—crowned peacocks and tufts of broom and the first word of his motto: "*Jamais [ne faillerai]*"—appear in the extremely original, discreetly elegant border of the frontispiece.

The scene depicts the same subject that decorates the beginning of the first version of the work (reproduced on the preceding Plate), but here it is treated in a completely different spirit. This time, the "Boucicaut Master" executed the work himself and handled it with special enthusiasm.

The figures have been clearly individualized; not only by their dress and emblems, but by their features. King Charles VI has been moved to the right of the picture; he is unceremoniously seated on the edge of his state bed, as though to indicate the intimate character of his conversation with Pierre Salmon. On the left, Jean sans Peur, Duke of Burgundy, is readily identifiable, as is the bareheaded Duke de Berry; the third man, who is holding the quarrel of a crossbow, could either be the Duke of Orléans or the Duke of Anjou.

This is one of the artist's best works, and he skillfully made use of the fleurs-de-lys-decorated curtains and draperies and of the chevroned rugs to create a three-dimensional space, whose rather precise perspective gives an illusion of depth. The open window at the back of the hall greatly contributes to the overall effect. In this connection we might mention the interior scenes which Fouquet painted later, in a famous copy of the *Grandes Chroniques de France*.

The "Boucicaut Master's" unchanging fascination with the minute objects of everyday life is expressed here by the flowerpot on the windowsill, but he also uses this detail to emphasize the skill with which he has opened the scene toward the exterior.

alemon quant tesfois et en pluseurs manieres
par braue experience de fait auons ueu et apperceu
le grant desir et la bonne boulente que bous auez
au bien de nous et de me royaume tant par les morales
auctoritez exemples et histoires a nous par bous alleguees

PLATE 31

THE BOOK OF WORLD WONDERS
fol. 97   *Pope John XXII Sends the Franciscan Oderic de Pordenone and his Companion James of Ireland to the Holy Land*

The taste of the great book lovers of the fourteenth and fifteenth centuries was not limited to manuscripts of a religious nature. Following the example set by King Charles V of France, they also encouraged the production of luxury volumes dealing with secular subjects; this required the exercise of great creative imagination on the part of the illustrators. Few works are as characteristic of this creativity as the famous *Book of Wonders*, offered to Jean de Berry in 1413 by his nephew Jean sans Peur, Duke of Burgundy.

The volume is a compilation of six totally different texts, composed at different periods by authors whose only common bond was their desire to gratify their contemporaries with their knowledge (either factual or imaginary) of countries that were almost unknown to Europeans at that time: the Near East, Africa, India, Central Asia, or China. The illustrators tried their best to depict faithfully whatever details of customs, costumes, or fauna in these distant regions they found in the texts, but naturally they had to rely largely upon imagination. Most of the time their love of the exotic led them far beyond the limits of reality, and even of probability.

The present painting is the frontispiece of an account by Oderic de Pordenone, a Franciscan friar whom Pope John XXII (1316–1334) sent to the Orient to preach the true faith to the infidels. He returned with a description of his travels, compiled in 1331.

Several artists, most probably from different workshops, collaborated on the abundant illustration of the volume. One easily recognizes the unique manner of the "Boucicaut Master" and his assistants (Plates 28 and 30), but a number of other paintings of an altogether different style relate to what Meiss called the "Bedford trend" (Plate 22). The Boucicaut workshop supplied large, airy compositions for the part of the volume entrusted to it—this page is a particularly good example—but their perfection was occasionally marred by a certain haste in the execution. The heavy foliage in the margins framing each frontispiece was, on the contrary, done in an entirely different style and could have been the work of a different workshop.

The arms of Jean de Berry in the center of the initial *C* were painted over the arms of Jean sans Peur, the original owner of the volume. The poly-lobed medallions punctuating the four corners of the border are of a much later period. They were added after the death of Jean de Berry, when the manuscript passed into other hands, notably those of Jacques d'Armagnac, Duke of Nemours.

y commence le chemin de la preginacion et du
voyage que fist vn bon homme de lordre des freres
meneurs. nomme frere odric de fose iulij. ne de vne
terre que on appelle port de veniſe qui par le comant
du pape ala oultre mer pour preſchier aur meſcre
ans la foy de dieu. Et ſont en ce liure contenu les
merueilles que li dis freres vit preſentement. et aul
ſy de pluſeurs autres leſquelles il oy compter en ces
pſties ſus dittes de gens dignes de foy. Mais celles quil oy racompter et
qial ne vit point. ne racompte il point pour vraie fors pour oir dire. et le ſo
ne en ſon langaige quant a ce vient. Et fu ce liure fait en latin par ce frere de
uant nomme en lan de grace mil. CCC. xxx. ptins le. xiij.e iour de ianuier

PLATE 32

THE ROHAN HOURS
fol. 27   *The Crucifixion*

This famous manuscript was probably executed between 1420 and 1427—in any case, after 1417. It owes its traditional denomination to its last owner, the Rohans, who had their arms repainted onto the pages; however, it had probably been ordered by Yolande of Aragon, from a workshop whose abundant productivity did not always result in exceptional quality.

A first-rate artist enriched the volume with several large full-page paintings, but left the margins to ofttimes mediocre collaborators who decorated them with scenes taken from the *Bible Moralisée*. There is no conclusive proof regarding his origins; he is sometimes thought to have been a Catalan, sometimes a native from Provence, but actually his deeply original genius cannot be confined to one specific milieu. His compositions—not too strong a word to use in his case—have breadth, and a strong sense of tragedy, not to say of the macabre. The pitiless realism with which he treated his intentionally oversized figures brought a completely new dimension and intensity to French illumination.

The *Crucifixion* reproduced here is perhaps less well known than the scenes of the *Judgment at Death* or the *Lamentation of the Virgin* (Plate 33). Its particular interest is that it represents a copy of an Italian illumination (in an altogether different stylistic interpretation) which treated the same subject in a *Bible Moralisée* called the *Anjou Bible* dating from the fourteenth century and belonging to the collection of Yolande of Aragon (Paris, Bibl. Nat. Ms. Fr. 9561, f. 178v). The Italian illumination served also as a guideline to the illuminators responsible for the marginal decorations in the *Rohan Hours*.

Despite their obvious kinship, the two paintings remain as dissimilar as Velasquez's *Menines* and Picasso's later interpretation of that painting. The colors used by the "Rohan Master" were totally different from those in the Italian model, and the flight of angels in the deep blue sky, which became a kind of trademark of the Rohan workshop, replaced the gold background found in the Italian model.

Moreover, a few original details have been added: the soul of the bad thief is carried off to hell by a demon, while an angel fiercely battles another demon for the soul of the good thief. This must be interpreted as a preoccupation with moralizing that is lacking in the archetype, but recurs in the *Judgment at Death*.

The features portrayed are often brutal, and even grimacing; they lack the grace evident in their models, but that makes them all the more dramatically expressive.

This master and his collaborators' decided taste for crowded compositions necessitated the addition of two extra figures on the left of the painting to rebalance the second, lower level of the image.

This is yet another example of how the original re-adaptation of previous models justifies the adjective currently used to characterize that style which, at the beginning of the fifteenth century, revitalized European illumination.

PLATE 33

THE ROHAN HOURS
fol. 135   *The Lamentation of the Virgin*

In this painting, the "Rohan Master" reached one of the pinnacles of his art. He was indeed never greater than in the dramatic rendering of grief and death.

We find here a most original combination of two different iconographic subjects: first, the Virgin swooning with grief in the arms of Saint John (a scene that is usually represented with Christ still on the Cross); and second, the body of Christ after He has been taken down from the Cross (often shown lying in His mother's lap).

The composition has been organized on a geometrical plan: Christ's bleeding body forms the basis of a right-angled triangle of which Saint John is the hypotenuse. Christ is shown in his nakedness, which emphasizes the wounds on his martyred body. The pitiful spectacle is more than the Virgin can bear: aged, dishevelled, arms dangling, she no longer has the strength to embrace her beloved Son, upon whose corpse she seems to fall, rather than throw herself.

The artist gave Saint John the same features as in his painting dedicated to Pentecost (f. 143 v). This extremely individualized face is also, more or less, the face of the dead man in the famous scene known as *The Judgment at Death* (f. 159); it has all the characteristics of a portrait painted after a live model. Turned toward God the Father, whose immense torso emerges from a firmament which legions of golden seraphs fill with a vast fluttering of wings, Saint John seems to express a bitter reproach. The Virgin's face is also shown in profile, but it is turned in the opposite direction, thus producing a striking contrast. In her grief, she cannot direct her eyes anywhere but to the ground upon which her Son's body is lying. Death is at this moment the only reality of which she is aware.

Despite the innumerable times each episode of the Passion has been depicted, one would look in vain through all of medieval illumination to find another composition that has achieved the same degree of gripping intensity.

34

PLATE 34

THE BREVIARY OF MARIE DE GUELDRE
fol. 19   *Marie de Gueldre Depicted as the Virgin Mary*

The colophon of this manuscript states that Marie, Duchess of Gueldre and Juliers, ordered this Breviary from the Augustinian monastery in Marienborn, near Arnhem, where it was completed in 1415. It is, nonetheless, a composite manuscript, written mainly in the dialect of the lower Rhineland, with several prayers in Dutch included toward the end.

Similarly, its decoration was the result of a collaboration by several artists. The painter responsible for the first part of the volume has been named the "Marie de Gueldre Master." The second part shows little homogeneity and is probably the work of two artists whose style closely resembles that of the workshop productions of the regular canons of Agnietenberg at Zwolle.

The page reproduced here probably has a very different origin and recalls the work done in the workshops of the Cologne area. Like the artist who painted the *Apotheosis of Giangaleazzo Visconti* (Plate 5), this painter has flattered his patron, Marie de Gueldre, so blatantly that it borders on the impious: he has placed her in an iconographic context normally reserved for paintings of the Annunciation.

In the upper part of the picture, God the Father sends a dove, symbol of the Holy Ghost, down to the young woman, who is shown standing in a flowering garden, enclosed by stone walls and espaliers *(hortus conclusus)*, the way the Virgin is often pictured. To stress the artist's intention even further, an angel carries a banderole with the inscription *"Ave Maria."* This strange composition probably expresses a wish for happy motherhood for Marie de Gueldre—a wish that, incidentally, remained unfulfilled.

Although composition and design were greatly inspired by Parisian models (themselves often the work of artists of Northern origin), color and technique denote the work of a Rhineland painter. It may be noted, however, that the beginning of the fifteenth century corresponded to the flowering of the "new style" in the Utrecht region.

PLATE 35

THE SACHSENSPIEGEL
fol. 20   *The Emperor Charlemagne Handing the Collection of Saxon Laws to "Duke" Widukind*

In 1220, Eike von Repkow compiled a Latin treatise or manual of civil and feudal Saxon laws entitled the *Sachsenspiegel*. The author himself translated it into Low German, and the work became rather widely read. As a reminder of the imperial capitulary of 797 which had introduced various legal dispositions in Saxony after its submission to Charlemagne, several copies of the *Sachsenspiegel* were decorated with a picture of the Emperor, handing the text—which was to be the law of the Saxon people—to the Saxon leader or "Duke" Widukind, whom he had defeated and compelled to accept baptism.

Saxon customs during the thirteenth century obviously consisted of many regulations relative to feudal institutions which Charlemagne, of necessity, had never imagined, but we know that the medieval spirit was not very sensitive to this type of anachronism. This beautiful copy of the Low German version of the *Sachsenspiegel* in Lüneburg contains only eleven decorated initials, apart from this frontispiece. The City of Lüneburg had it undertaken by local artists for its own use, and the volume is known to have been completed in 1405. Reinecke attributed the decoration to the artist of the *Golden Table* which is kept at the Church of Lüneburg; the *Wesselhoven Missal* is, in all probability, another work by the same artist.

This unique illumination is painted on a gold background, a tradition that continued longest outside of France. It shows Charlemagne handing the Saxon Code to Widukind, surrounded by his companions, whom the artist has depicted as notables of Lüneburg. As an additional anachronism he included the author of the *Sachsenspiegel* in his composition (whose name appears in an inscription). In the lower margin we note the arms of the City of Lüneburg (a triple-turreted portal), and those of the principality of the same name (a "lion rampant"). Acanthus shoots winding around a golden staff complete the marginal decoration.

The disposition of the platform and the baldachin have created a skillful illusion of depth; the painting is the work of a fine artist who may be compared to "Meister Francke" and Konrad von Soest.

PLATE 36

THE BIBLE OF PETER GRILLINGER
fol. 3   *Saint Rupert and the Canon Grillinger*

It took Johann Freibeck of Königsbrück two years to copy the enormous Bible commissioned by Peter Grillinger, a Salzburg Canon, who offered it to the Cathedral of his town in 1430.

It was decorated with two full-page paintings, one of which—the one reproduced here—appears at the beginning of the volume and represents Saint Rupert, Patron Saint of Salzburg.

Seated on a throne and wearing episcopal dress, the Saint blesses Canon Peter Grillinger who is kneeling before him, reciting the prayer inscribed on the banderole on the right: *Intercede pro me, Sancte Ruperte* ("Saint Rupert, intercede for me").

Behind the Saint, angels hold up a large gold-embroidered tapestry—a frequent iconographic cliché. The gold background belongs to a decorative tradition that remained in favor much longer in the east of Europe than in France. Also noteworthy is the importance given to the architectural baldachin which occupies the upper part of the painting. It may be compared to the baldachin above the Emperor Charlemagne in the *Sachsenspiegel* of Lüneburg (Plate 35).

The marginal framework, composed of a rod wound about with plant shoots, punctuated by monkeys, birds, and masks, is of the most sparing elegance.

PLATE 37

THE SHERBORNE MISSAL
fol. 380   *The Crucifixion*

In all probability, this Missal was executed at the Benedictine Abbey of Saint Mary of Sherborne, in Dorsetshire, and for the Abbey's own use.

Consequently, this is not the product of a commercial workshop, as were most luxury manuscripts executed at that time throughout Europe (and particularly in France). This Missal was, nonetheless, a collective undertaking. Several artists collaborated on it; the most interesting — who probably assumed the responsibility for the project as a whole — made himself known (in a display of rather exceptional pride). He belonged to the Dominican order of Friars, and called himself John Siferwas, Syfewas, or Siferwast.

It is all the more interesting to note, in a volume of strictly monastic origin and destination, the influence of artistic trends that were, at that time, evident in the Rhineland and in Bohemia, and which contributed greatly to the renaissance of English illumination of that period. It is, moreover, not impossible that Richard II of England's marriage to Anne of Bohemia may have attracted artists from Central Europe to England, who would have brought their models with them and thus helped spread a fashion. At any rate, it cannot be denied that *The Sherborne Missal* shows obvious stylistic analogies with *The Bible of King Wenceslas* (Plate 10). Millar nonetheless hesitates to attribute a definite origin to the "new style." He is inclined to think that the Rhineland region was its most likely source, but not without a certain measure of influence from the Franco-Flemish and Dutch schools of the time.

The *Crucifixion* reproduced here can, in fact, rightfully be linked to certain paintings of the Cologne school, and also to the *Crucifixion of Darmstadt*, which dates from around 1440 and has been attributed to the Middle Rhineland; in the latter, just as in the present instance, the bad thief turns his back on the main group.

We may agree with Turner that *The Sherborne Missal* is the first important truly English example of the International Gothic Style, even though its design and modeling are reminiscent of the "East-Anglian" tradition.

38

PLATE 38

THE BEAUFORT HOURS
fol. 23 v   *The Annunciation*

This important Book of Hours produced in England a few years after 1401 may have
been intended for John of Beaufort, first Count of Somerset, and his wife, Margaret of
Holland. The volume owes its name to this plausible attribution, but other opinions
affirm that its first owner may have been John, first Duke of Somerset, the husband of
Margaret de Beauchamp.

D. H. Turner considers *The Beaufort Hours* a typical example of "International Art" in
the field of illumination, since the decoration was most likely the work of foreign artists.
We can distinguish at least two, if not three hands, which is not surprising, since the
elements composing the manuscript differ as to dates. T. C. Skeat has shown that the
twelve paintings preceding the text of the actual Book of Hours might well have come
from an English Psalter (kept today in Reims). According to him, the painting reproduced here has the same origin, although a few years earlier.

This *Annunciation* is certainly the best page in the entire volume. It is most often
attributed to Herman Scheere, an artist who undoubtedly came from the Netherlands,
or from the Rhineland, and who signed illuminations of a very similar composition
around the same period. (It is interesting to note that the inscription on the drapery of
the prie-dieu upon which the Virgin is leaning [*Omnia levia sunt amanti. Si quis amat non
laborat* . . . —"All is easy when one loves. He who loves labors not . . ."] recurs in two
other manuscripts—one of them *The Breviary of the Archbishop of Chichele*—followed by
the name "Herman." This probably indicates that the inscription was a kind of
workshop motto.) It must be pointed out, however, that this attribution has not met
with universal agreement.

The influence of the famous retable by Melchior Broederlam (Dijon, Musée des
Beaux Arts) upon this *Annunciation* is evident, no matter who the artist may have been.
This fact demonstrates England's interest in the "new style" that was evolving on the
continent.

39

PLATE 39

CHAUCER: TROILUS AND CRISEYDE
fol. 1 v   *The Author Reads his Work before an Elegant Audience*

The decoration of this particularly fine manuscript of Chaucer's *Troilus and Criseyde* was begun in the south of England during the very beginning of the fifteenth century. It was to have been embellished with a great number of paintings for which the scribe had allowed the necessary space on the designated pages, but for some unknown reason the project was never completed.

This is all the more regrettable since the frontispiece alone provides an excellent example of the artistic quality of English illuminators, especially when dealing with nonreligious subjects. At the time, their style had been undergoing a profound renewal, and the present reproduction is a fine demonstration of their careful attention to the so-called International Style flowering then on the continent.

This large composition shows the poet reading his work from behind a kind of lectern in the open air, for the enjoyment of a large although select, audience. It was visibly inspired by Franco-Flemish influences.

The castle in the background recalls the buildings which Jean de Berry's painters were fond of placing in the background of their compositions, in the same lateral manner. The landscape with its steep rocks also recalls Italianate models, and the trees are treated in the same synthetic manner as at the bottoms of the pages in the *Très Belles Heures de Notre Dame*. The two women in the bottom left-hand corner of the painting seem to have come from one of the Boccaccio manuscripts that were illustrated in Paris around 1400 (Plate 16). They could also be compared to the two flower-picking young girls in the betrothal scene of the *Très Riches Heures* (Plate 26).

The border which frames the painting is, on the contrary, absolutely English, as evidenced by the motifs which appear there, as well as by its colors. The use of a gold background was quite rare on the continent at the time; one does, nevertheless, find some such examples in French manuscripts that were probably inspired by Bohemian models.

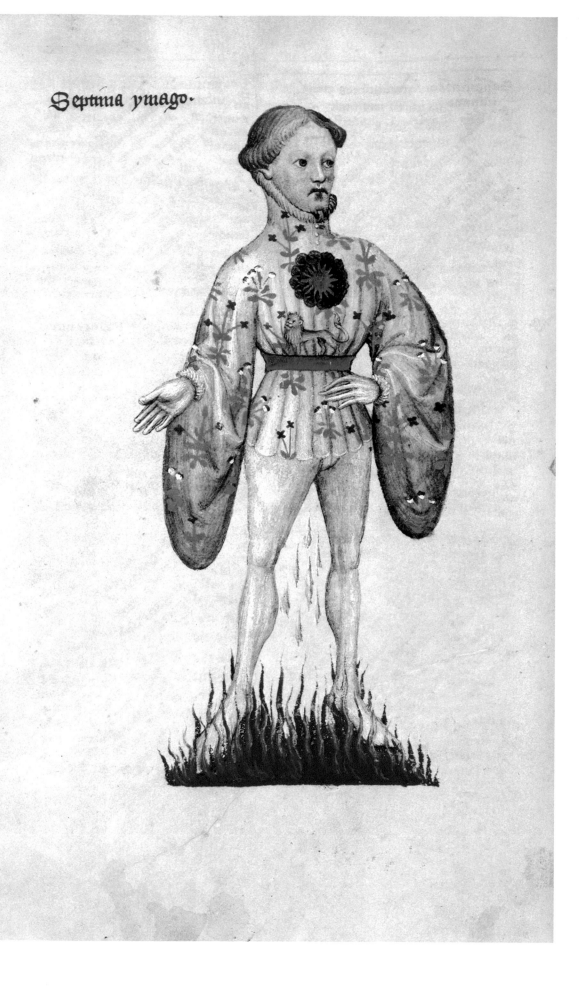

PLATE 40

JOHN FOXTON: LIBER COSMOGRAPHIAE
fol. 35 v   *The Sun*

An inscription at the end of the present manuscript gives John Foxton the title of chaplain *(capellanus)*. In 1408 he offered this copy of his work to the Trinitarians of the Convent of Saint Robert near Knaresborough in Yorkshire.

This was a vast compilation, dealing with astronomy (or rather astrology), history, and medicine. It was accompanied by a number of diagrams and tables, and especially by twelve beautiful paintings similar to the present reproduction. Four of them represented the human "temperaments": sanguine, phlegmatic, melancholic, and choleric. A "Zodiacal Man" showed the influence of the Zodiac on the various parts of the body, in keeping with the theory that was generally accepted during the Middle Ages; the Limbourgs gave an admirable representation of it in the *Très Riches Heures*. The last seven paintings were devoted to the seven planets known at that time; they were shown as human beings, whose garments bore the emblems of the heavenly bodies they represented, as well as the corresponding zodiacal symbols.

Two artists were responsible for this series of paintings. One of them has been identified as the master who created the illustrations for a treatise by Thomas Hoccleve now in the British Library. The style of the other is similar to that of the famous Herman Scheere (Plate 38), and, just like his work, shows the influence of Bohemian art.

The present painting was the seventh in the planetary series. The sun is personified here by a young man wearing a rich garment embroidered with flowers; above the belt, a lion symbolizes the zodiacal sign of the same name. On his chest appears a golden sun in the form of a medallion; it is not suspended on a chain and seems to be attached to the garment. The flames that lick the young man's feet without burning them recall the nature of the sun, dispenser of warmth and light.